On the Trail of Jack the Ripper

On the Trail of Jack the Ripper

Richard Charles Cobb
&
Mark Davis

PEN & SWORD
HISTORY

First published in Great Britain in 2022 by
Pen & Sword History
An imprint of
Pen & Sword Books Ltd
Yorkshire – Philadelphia

Copyright © Richard Charles Cobb 2022

ISBN 978 1 52679 478 9

Printed in the UK by CPI Group (UK) Ltd, Croydon, CR0 4YY.

Pen & Sword Books Limited incorporates the imprints of Atlas, Archaeology,
Aviation, Discovery, Family History, Fiction, History, Maritime, Military, Military
Classics, Politics, Select, Transport, True Crime, Air World, Frontline Publishing,
Leo Cooper, Remember When, Seaforth Publishing, The Praetorian Press,
Wharncliffe Local History, Wharncliffe Transport, Wharncliffe True Crime
and White Owl.

For a complete list of Pen & Sword titles please contact

PEN & SWORD BOOKS LIMITED
47 Church Street, Barnsley, South Yorkshire, S70 2AS, England
E-mail: enquiries@pen-and-sword.co.uk
Website: www.pen-and-sword.co.uk

Or

PEN AND SWORD BOOKS
1950 Lawrence Rd, Havertown, PA 19083, USA
E-mail: Uspen-and-sword@casematepublishers.com
Website: www.penandswordbooks.com

Contents

Acknowledgments		vi
Foreword		vii
Introduction		xi
Chapter 1	The Whitechapel Murders Begin	1
Chapter 2	Mary Ann Nichols	13
Chapter 3	Annie Chapman	28
Chapter 4	Ripper Land	43
Chapter 5	Dear Boss –	56
Chapter 6	The Double Event – Elizabeth Stride	61
Chapter 7	The Double Event – Catherine Eddowes	72
Chapter 8	Discovery at Goulston Street	83
Chapter 9	From Hell	91
Chapter 10	Mary Jane Kelly	97
Chapter 11	Were There Other Victims?	114
Chapter 12	So Who Was He?	123

Acknowledgments

Many thanks to all who have supported, encouraged and aided this book into being. Thanks in particular to the unwavering support of my family, my parents and brothers and my close friends who never tire of me going on about this gruesome but fascinating subject.

A special thanks to author, historian and close friend, Neil R. Storey, who wrote the superb foreword for our book.

Also to Chris Clark, Steve Blomer, Elizabeth Blakemore, Scott Nichol, Mel Simpson, Mick Priestley, Ashlin Orell, Fiona Kay, John Chambers, Vikki Roberts, Kirsty Giles, Sinnead O'Leary, Andre Price, John Holloway, Lindsey Siviter, Anjum Fi, Edward Stow, Zara Liddle, Trish Routh, Karen and Martin Trueman, David Jones, Luka Hirst, Amy Harper, Liva Andruce, Breen Lynch, Bernie Conroy and all the staff at the White Hart Pub, Aldgate East.

Finally it's no exaggeration to say that this book would never have been possible without the help and guidance of historians Mr Rob Clack and Mr Chris Routh. The images, photographs, maps and diagrams, that no doubt will impress all who read this book, have been beautifully put together and collected over the years by these two fantastic researchers and friends. Many thanks to both of you.

Foreword

by Neil R. Storey

Men go and come, but earth abides.

Ecclesiastes 1:4

One of the sets of books that I treasure above all is the one that consists of three tall green volumes with elegant gilt titling that are Living *London: Its Work and Its Play. It's Humour and Its Pathos. Its Sights and Its Scenes* edited by the ebullient journalist, editor, playwright and novelist George R. Sims. Treasured not least because they were kindly given to me by my dear friend Stewart Evans many years ago when I was beginning to explore the wider context of the crimes and times of Jack the Ripper. The gift of those books was not just a generous one but one that has provided me with so many insights into those times. Published in the first years of the twentieth century, the superbly illustrated pages and evocative text capture so much of the city, good and bad, from the magnificence of State occasions and theatre life to the misery of slums and criminal types, by those who observed them first hand in the closing years of the nineteenth century.

Living London were not the first volumes nor would they be the last books of their kind. London has always been a changing and dynamic city, one of its first popular histories was published by antiquarian Thomas Pennant in 1790. As the nineteenth century progressed and the city was redeveloped, there was little or no consideration given to the preservation of historic buildings. Antiquarians, authors and historians saw how rapidly the city was changing and sought to highlight significant historic buildings and monuments that were in danger of being swept away and lost forever in the name of progress. As a result some were saved. Sadly, some were not.

By the late nineteenth century London was the beating heart of the British Empire, one of the most wide spread and powerful empires the world had ever seen. Despite all the riches that this brought, bitter poverty of the worst kind was still rife in the metropolis. More disturbing still, it was often literally around the corner from the fine frontages of houses on busy streets because the yards and tenements off the alleyways that ran beside them were the cramped, damp, filthy and Disease-ridden tenements inhabited by people and families in poverty. The East End was no exception; in fact it was the worst area of poverty and degradation in London. Indeed the decline of those who fell on hard times could often be marked as they moved from the more affluent areas of the capital to the cheapest, most down-at-heel areas of the East, into workhouses and even living on the streets.

Before the days of mass media or well-illustrated newspapers many lived quite insular lives outside the capital, happy to live out their days in the village or town where they were born and a trip to their local market town was considered quite an event. Many never even contemplated a visit to London and were ignorant of the depths of poverty there. Tragically, many of those who were aware of it and who were in a position to make a difference chose, in a very Victorian fashion, to ignore the poverty stricken and pretend they did not exist. Out of sight, out of mind.

Not all turned away; Salvation Army founder William Booth was among those who wanted to make a difference and founded the East London Christian Mission back in 1865. Despite his efforts and the good work of others it took *The Bitter Cry of Outcast London* by Andrew Mears and William C. Preston to strike the first chord to raise national concern. Originally published as an anonymous penny pamphlet in 1883 its impact was described just two years later as having: '*rang through the length and breadth of the land. It touched the hearts of tens of thousands, and awoke deep feelings of indignation, pain, and sympathy in every direction.*'

Charles Booth (no relation to William) and his team of researchers began their survey of life and labour in London in 1886. Their work not only evolved into numerous volumes of findings but also the remarkable 'poverty maps' of the city. Seven colour codes were allotted for each street or areas within the street that ranged from yellow marking those of the wealthy upper classes, red for middling sorts and well-to-do down to light blue for those scraping by, dark blue for those who were poor and in 'chronic want' to black for the lowest class of those considered 'vicious' and 'semi-criminal.' Graphically proving to anyone who cared to see for themselves on these detailed maps that in the East End poverty was their neighbour and there were some of the blackest streets of London within its bounds.

Against this social backdrop occurred a series of murders during the Autumn of 1888 that were so horrific they were claimed to have made the people of London walk in terror. No wonder when the killer was depicted as a knife wielding phantom by John Tenniel in *Punch* on 29 September 1888 the cartoon was entitled '*The Nemesis of Neglect.*' However, the killer who had been described in the press up to that date as the 'Whitechapel Murderer' claimed his own nom de plume in a letter received by the Central News Agency on 27 September 1888. Known after its opening line as the 'Dear Boss' letter it was signed 'Jack the Ripper.'

Despite almost certainly being the invention of a press reporter the name engendered that *something* that creates a perfect storm capturing the imagination of both press and public. The unprecedented, shocking nature of the murders and the fact that they were never solved ensured this was a name that would live on in infamy. Perhaps, just as a bogeyman that parents would use to threaten children when not wanting them to wander off or when they misbehaved, warning 'Jack the Ripper will get you!'

However, it did not end there. This most infamous series of unsolved murders attracted a huge amount of conjecture over the identity of the killer, hundreds of letters shared concerns and suspicions of the identity of the murderer with the police and amateur detectives attempted to track down the killer at the time of the murders and beyond. What a coup that would have been for the person who positively identified and brought about the successful conviction of Jack the Ripper! Even though enough time has now passed for us all to be certain that Jack is long dead, the search still goes on and every year a new suspect, account of the crimes or stories of the victims are published. Even over a century after the murders each new generation that comes along encounters the story somewhere, be it on film, television, books, magazines, newspapers or online. Although for some it comes as quite a shock to discover the murders of Jack the Ripper were only too real and Sherlock Holmes is a fictional character.

The crimes and times of Jack the Ripper, especially the iconic image of the top hatted 'gentleman' killer swathed in a long black cape disappearing into the London of dark alleyways, gas lamps and smog is one which seduces thousands of people from across Britain and around the world to make the journey to London and see the murder sites for themselves every year. The problem which emerges for some visitors, or those planning a visit, is they may gather the impression that the London of Jack the Ripper has been swept away. To a certain extent this is true and the murder sites themselves have all changed beyond recognition. However, there are still some cobbled streets and Victorian style lamps in the East End of London. Despite blitz, wrecking ball demolition and developers all taking their toll there are still plenty of touchstones, buildings and features that remain. Some of them can be spotted quite easily, others require a good guide to show them to you and share their stories.

Many of us who have researched London in the past have come across a gem of a documentary entitled '*The London that Nobody Knows*' made in 1967. It is based on the book of the same title by London historian Geoffrey Fletcher, a man who saw the old London and its people that would have been recognised by George R. Sims in his book '*Living London*' were fading fast and set about recording them in words and pictures before it was too late. The documentary, eloquently presented by James Mason, captures that time perfectly along with some of the people and atmosphere of the place, including a visit to the Jack the Ripper murder site in the back yard of 29, Hanbury Street. Mason comments thoughtfully that the place had hardly changed since 1888. The site clung on for a handful of years after the film but the yard and the houses were demolished and are now gone forever. The houses featured on Fornier Street with their railings and fine frontages that looked so rotten and beyond hope on the film, however, have been beautifully restored and now change hands for millions. Such is fate.

Richard Cobb is a man who has researched the East End and London of Jack the Ripper, he has lived and worked in the East End, he knows its stories and people today and draws on all of that knowledge to create this book. His text is accompanied by some superb photographs of Victorian London then and now. Very much in the same spirit of 'The London that Nobody Knows' Richard recounts the Ripper story and captures the essence of the place today, albeit the places where the shadow of the Ripper still lingers.

Introduction

"Spitalfields is Jack the Ripper territory"
James Mason – The London Nobody knows 1968

Let's start by acknowledging the fact that we will probably never know the identity of history's most elusive serial killer. Well, not to everyone's satisfaction at least. The police did not catch him. They have variously been called incompetent or party to a conspiracy or cover-up. It's even claimed the police knew who it was but it was someone so important that they could not reveal it to the public.

Thus is the fantasy and romance that surrounds the most infamous murder mystery in the world. But in truth, the reason they never caught Jack the Ripper is

A view up Whitechapel High Street in the late 1800's. The church in the distance marking the centre of Whitechapel

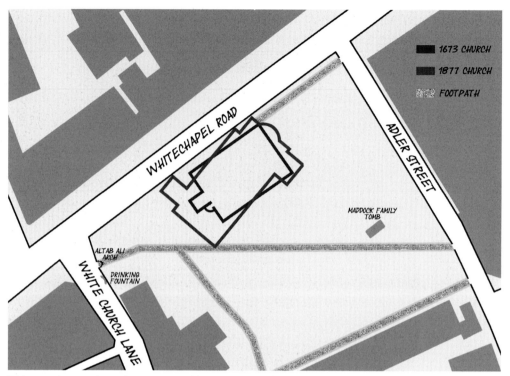

Diagram showing how the structure of St Mary Matfelon changed over the years.

because they lacked the experience. They were dealing with a new type of killer, the first of his kind, the world's first modern serial killer. The police were simply not equipped to hunt him down. They closed the investigation down after four years, (although the last record attached to it was in 1896) leaving the case unsolved. They also were under extreme pressure, both from a highly critical press and an equally criticised government who were demanding action. Finally, they did not have the resources or technology at their disposal that a modern police investigation would. There were no forensic examinations, DNA or fingerprints that could be used in an 1888 police investigation. Today London is one of the most surveillanced cities in the world. If Jack was running around modern Whitechapel, I am fairly confident he would have been caught quite easily by camera alone, never mind police techniques.

The term "serial killer" is one with which we are now familiar. The phenomenon is not a new one, but the term itself is recent and did not exist 50 years ago, never mind 130 years ago. Federal Bureau of Investigation agent and member of the FBI psychological profiling team Robert Ressler is often credited for coining the term "serial killer" in the 1970's, to describe those that murder several victims, obsessively, and often with a deviant sexual motive.

A modern seating area in Altab Ali Park maps out the where the original church once stood.

Before then, a killer who murdered in this way was known as a "mass murderer." Today we characterise killers differently, for instance the "mass murderer" is now someone who kills four or more people at the same time (or in a short period of time) in the same place, and then we have "spree killers", who murder randomly over multiple locations and usually within a short period of time.

Serial killers are different, they often work alone, and they have no attachment or connection to their victims and pretty much kill for the sake of killing. Today they are generally defined to be someone who kills three or more people, one at a time, over a relatively short period.

Jack the Ripper is regarded as the father of the modern day Serial Killer as he is the first early example of this type of murderer. He was not a prolific killer: he is thought to have murdered five victims, more or less, and here begins the enduring mystery which has captured the imagination of the world.

Many other British serial killers have murdered more. These notorious criminals are, unfortunately, household names, for example Peter Sutcliffe, Dennis Nilsen, Harold Shipman, and the serial killing couple, Fred and Rose West

Peter Sutcliffe, usually attacking his victims from behind with a hammer, killed 13 but attempted to murder a further seven. Carrying out his attacks and murders in the north of England between 1975 and 1981, he is better known as the "Yorkshire Ripper."

Dennis Nilsen, "the Kindly Killer", murdered 15 young men between 1978 and 1983. Fred West, with his wife Rose, killed at least 12, but before committing suicide in 1995 he admitted there were more. Harold Shipman, also known as "Doctor Death," murdered his patients, probably in excess of 250, from 1975 to 1998.

Serial killers fascinate and repel and none more so than the case of Jack the Ripper. Here we see a difference. He, strangely enough, remains the only serial killer in history to define an actual era. When you mention his name anywhere in the world, you instantly think of Victorian London, foggy nights, horse and carriages, gas lamps and that lone top hat wearing figure lurking in a dark alley way. If anything the Ripper is as much part of Victorian London as Queen Victoria herself.

The struggle to identify him has remained the favourite pastime of retired policemen, crime writers and jaded historians for the last 133 years. We have been beset by theories that the Ripper was a barrister, an evil doctor, a mad polish Jew or even an insane Royal Prince. The real truth will almost certainly never be known.

Poverty and homelessness was rife in the East End of London. Each night, hundreds of men and women would seek shelter in over cramped Doss Houses

The Ripper's long appeal lies with 130 years of books, movies, plays and references in pop culture. Those years have twisted the mental image of the killer into a real life gothic bogeyman, on the same level as fictional villains like Freddy Kruger and Michael Myers. His fictional costume will forever be the long dark cloak, the top hat, white gloves and doctor's bag. It is this myth that has kept the public's fascination going for so long.

The myth, however, is a million miles from reality.

Even today if you ask anyone how many victims Jack the Ripper claimed, you will usually get an answer that ranges from just a few unfortunate individuals to hundreds of potential victims. There is a simple reason for this – nobody actually knows the answer. The killer was never caught so his true death toll will never be known.

As far as the police were concerned, the murders spanned three years (1888-1891) and included a proposed eleven victims: Emma Smith, Martha Tabram, Mary Ann Nichols, Annie Chapman, Elizabeth Stride, Catherine Eddowes, Mary Jane Kelly, Rose Mylett, Alice McKenzie, Frances Coles and one unfortunate, unidentified headless torso. All these identified women were known to be local prostitutes living in common lodging houses in a relatively small area.

In 1894, Melville Macnaghten, former Chief Constable of the Metropolitan Police, wrote a private memorandum in which he claimed that "the Whitechapel murderer had five victims and five victims only"

These five victims – Nichols, Chapman, Stride, Eddowes and Kelly – have become known as the 'Canonical Five'. The similarity in the way they were killed (throats cut, abdominal mutilations and, in three cases, internal organs removed) suggests that this idea is a sound one, but it does have its detractors.

When looking at contemporary reports in the press, we then notice that after the murder of Nichols in August 1888, many felt that the previous deaths of Emma Smith (April 1888) and Martha Tabram (August 1888), could also have been the work of the same hand and thus, at the time, Nichols was considered the third victim.

Put simply, the Whitechapel Murders spanned eleven victims over three years, but the one individual known as Jack the Ripper is widely thought to be responsible for the Canonical Five killings in a ten-week period later labelled as the 'Autumn of Terror'.

So just as you have the mystery of who was this elusive fiend and how many did he kill, you also have the perfect setting for this great Victorian mystery – Whitechapel -London's East End

These days, the East End is known for its diverse population and multi-culturalism as much as it is for being a working class tourist destination. With a

Brick lane 2021

history that is just as vivacious as the present day with visible throwbacks to days gone by – those cobblestones, the Borough has made leaps and bounds over the last century.

Rewind to the year 1888 and you'll be presented with a very different depiction of the East End, especially in Whitechapel. The name for this infamous quarter originally came from a small local chapel, St Mary's, which later developed into the local church of St Mary Matfelon. Nobody really knows how long this original church was standing in the area but we start getting a mention of it around the 1300's. Over the centuries the church was rebuilt several times with the last version surviving into the 1940's but sadly destroyed in a blitz attack during the war. After lying derelict for many years it was eventually demolished. Modern visitors to the area can still visit the site where it once stood. All that remains of the old church is a modern day outline of the floor plan and a few scattered graves. It is now known as Altab Ali park (named after a 25 year old British Bangladeshi clothing worker who was sadly murdered in the area in 1978).

Apart from this not much is really known about Whitechapel until around the 16th century when we do start to see evidence of a class divide. Up until then the area was quite rural, but following the great fire of London in 1666 traders and businesses started to expand out beyond the city walls. Brick and tile manufacturers really took off on the back of the fire, where the old method of wood and thatch houses were replaced with a much stronger – and slightly more fire resistant – option. Understandably the area where these businesses operated soon became known as Brick Lane.

With the success of the new enterprises and the markets such as Spitalfields this attracted more people into the area. French Huguenots fleeing persecution brought their silk weaving skills to London and the impressive houses they worked from can still be seen in and around streets such as Fournier Street.

The French were soon followed by the Irish linen makers, who also helped in building up the London dockland. As the area grew in popularity, Spitalfields became a parish in its own right in 1729 when Hawksmoor Christ church was consecrated.

The 1820's saw a sharp decline in Spitalfields as it gained a reputation for being a really cheap place to live so close to the city. After the Irish we then see the arrival of the eastern Europeans and the Jewish community escaping the Polish pogroms and the harsh conditions in Russia. It was now on course to become unbearably overcrowded. Such was the mass influx of immigration that between the 1880's and 1970's we see that Spitalfields was overwhelmingly Jewish with over 40 synagogues. Today we see the area has shifted once again to a more Bengali community.

As industry expanded certain areas of the East End were not regulated by London rules. They also were far enough outside of the city, away from the relatively well-to-do central London residents, to create perfect homes for some unpleasant and noxious businesses.

London needed industries like tanning, brewing, abattoirs and foundries. Understandably the people living within the city preferred not to have these industries located within the walls. Many of the factories produced noxious, and often dangerous, smells. Many sprang up in the East End in areas like Whitechapel, where they were close enough to service the rest of London, but not close enough to smell or see!

By the time Jack the Ripper was about to emerge, Whitechapel was seedy by any standards, it was a crime-ridden sordid quarter, where 78,000 residents lived in abject poverty. It was now an area of mainly doss houses, sweatshops, abattoirs, overcrowded slums, pubs, a few shops and warehouses, leavened with a row or two of respectably kept cottages. A hive of criminals, prostitutes, layabouts and gangs; everywhere you looked was tinged with disease, despair and alcoholism.

Squalid living conditions made these cramped quarters even worse. With so many people around and so few job opportunities, it is easy to see why so many turned to gang-related crime and prostitution.

According to one account, the women of the East End at the time were so destitute that they would sell themselves for as little as four pence, or a stale loaf of bread. In October 1888, the Metropolitan Police estimated there were just over 1,200 prostitutes working the streets in Whitechapel alone. This was almost certainly an underestimate, for sheer want drove many more to occasional prostitution.

This was their only means of income and survival. With the little money they earned, most would seek comfort in alcohol as the only refuge from reality. Drink was cheap and drunkenness rife, at any

A modern resident of Whitechapel in 2021 rests against the back drop of Jack the Ripper's London.

time of day or night, leading to brutality and violence as a direct result. Brawls were commonplace and, as one Whitechapel inhabitant put it, cries of "Murder!" were "nothing unusual in the street."

The Hollywood interpretation of these fallen women has them portrayed as the showgirl type you would see on a stage in the rich West End, with charming looks and pretty features. The reality was far different. By the age of 20, most would look about 40, due to hard drinking and the East End lifestyle taking its toll. Most had missing teeth and wore the same clothes day in and day out. Bloated and diseased, life would have been short for these women. Dubbed 'Unfortunates,' these women would ply their trade within brothels and dark alleys. London's West End may have thrived in the Victorian period, but the East End was drowning.

This small area became the killer's hunting ground and interestingly, it is actually one of the few serial killer cases where you can walk to all the crime scenes in less than two hours. But it was a small world in which Jack the Ripper would have no problem finding a victim.

But on the other side of the coin, the murders would thrust the East End into the spotlight. As a direct result of the publicity directed at Whitechapel by the Jack the Ripper murders, the process of slum clearance was speeded up and numerous charitable institutions of social aid in Victorian times were set up in the area. The crimes did more than 50 years of agitation to improve the lot of the poor and destitute. They also attracted support and members to the socialist political parties and to the growing trade unions.

The murders would also change the way the police handled these cases going forward. It set a precedent for how not to handle such cases with regards to recording, investigation and evidence. It also started the love/hate relationship that can be seen today between the police and the press, thanks to the sensationalised stories that were printed by the tabloids of the time.

It is only when you put Jack the Ripper and London at the time into context that you can see how this is considered the greatest murder mystery of all time and how the story will (whether you like it or not) live on forever.

But what remains from the Ripper's London today and what more can we learn from this story?

"Jack the Ripper's London? Surely it's all gone, nothing exists anymore." I hear you say. Well at first glance it might appear that nothing of Jack the Ripper's London has survived, but I assure you those little pockets of Victorian history are still everywhere you look in our modern world. In fact the idea for this book was based on giving those curious modern travellers a glimpse of the past and to show them that there are still sections of London's East End that have changed little since the Autumn of 1888.

On any given night in Whitechapel, scores of tourists will flock to take part in Jack the Ripper tours and hopefully capture the atmosphere of what it must have been like to live through one of London's most infamous periods of history. For ten years, I and several other guides have been conducting the famous Ripper-Vision tour in Whitechapel, hoping to educate and (in a strange way) entertain those who dare to journey into the back streets of London after dark in search of history's most elusive villain. Along the way we use the murders to also highlight the fascinating history of the East End, where it's been, how it came about and where it is going. Because above all else the Ripper story is just a small piece of a much larger social jigsaw which should never be forgotten.

This book will investigate primarily the five canonical victims, giving the reader a greater insight into each murder, how and where it happened, plus what became of the sites in the decades to follow. We will also include the other Whitechapel murders which are often ignored by modern investigators. At the same time we give the reader a glimpse into the past whilst acknowledging what is going on in Jack the Ripper's London of today.

We hope this will give the reader a better understanding of the crimes and the area and allow the reader to make up their own mind about what actually happened in the East End of London more than 130 years ago.

They say a picture paints a thousand words but visiting the actual crime scene paints a million. Here you get a real grasp of the events that unfolded at the time. It's an invaluable tool that all crime scene investigators need in order to reach their conclusion.

So with this in mind, it's time for us to visit the crime scenes and surrounding areas for the first time in over 130 years. Taking all the eye witness reports, police statements and files from the Home Office and armed with a trusty camera, we find ourselves back on the trail of Jack the Ripper.

Chapter 1

The Whitechapel Murders Begin

"A serial killer does not emerge fully formed. Even he must learn his craft –
and Jack learned quickly".

Edward Buchan – Whitechapel

The Whitechapel murders actually began four months before the first
accepted Jack the Ripper murder took place, with Emma Elizabeth Smith
who passed away at the London Hospital at 9.00am on the morning of
4 April 1888. Much of her life is a mystery, but no more so than the circumstances
of her death. She was a resident of 18 George Street, Spitalfields, a low lodging
house, and was believed to be a prostitute, one of the many who frequented the area
and its doss-houses. Some accounts claimed she was a widow with two children

Osborn Street 2021.

living in Finsbury Park, then a neat suburb of London, and had once had a much better life than the one she had descended into in the mean streets of the East End. What is known for sure is that the cause of her death was peritonitis, the result of shocking injuries inflicted on her the previous day.

The previous Easter Monday, 2 April, Smith had stuck to her regular routine, leaving her lodging house at around 6.00pm. It is believed she would work the streets and return in the early hours of the following morning, where she would often find herself the worse for wear after getting involved in drunken brawls. On this particular evening, she made her way to Poplar where the Bank Holiday customers in the dockside pubs would become potential clients. It turned out to be a rather fruitless and dangerous evening; Smith was seen with a man around 12.15am by fellow prostitute Margaret Hayes on Burdett Road, not long before Hayes herself was beaten by some men and decided to call it a night. The next time anybody officially saw Emma Smith was when she walked into her lodging house in great pain and distress.

As she had been making her way home, Smith claimed to have been followed from Whitechapel High Street to Brick Lane by a group of three men, who set about her near the junction with Wentworth Street. The exact location of the

The Junction of Brick Lane and Osborn Street where Emma Smith was attacked by 3 men on 3 April 1888.

Could one of Emma Smith's attackers have gone on to become Jack the Ripper?

attack is somewhat of a mystery. According to police reports the attack took place on a pathway opposite number 10 Brick Lane. Other reports say it was opposite the cocoa and mustard factory, south west corner of Wentworth and Osborn Street. The distance between these locations is only 15 yards so there is room for error on both accounts.

She was beaten, robbed, possibly raped and then had a blunt instrument thrust into her vagina with great force. It was several hours before she appeared in George Street, yet there were no reports of any sightings of her. Mary Russell and Annie Lee took Smith to the London Hospital where she was seen by Dr George Haslip, and there she proceeded to recount the assault. Gradually, Smith would slip into a coma, as the injury to the vagina had ruptured the perineum, causing a dangerous infection and resulting in Smith passing away early the next morning.

The East End had seen many outrages and tragedies, but this was thought of as being particularly brutal. Nobody was brought to justice over the affair, and many commentators felt this was indicative of a growing audacity and violence within the gang culture of the area. Some of these gangs were known to prey on prostitutes as they were vulnerable and all evidence (though there was little) put the attack on Smith in this category. But it is difficult to know if Emma Smith's story is totally accurate. Some have suggested that she may have been set upon by a loner or a

The White Hart Pub 2021.

violent pimp and that she used the gang story to deflect attention from her role as a prostitute.

From the evidence we have this seems like a clear case of robbery by one of the local gangs, possibly the Old Nichol gang who had a well-known reputation for attacking prostitutes. In his book "East London", written only eleven years after the murders, Walter Besant wrote:

Hustling people in the street is natural. The boys gather together and hold the street; if anyone ventures to pass through it they rush upon him, knock him down, and kick him savagely about the head; they rob him as well. In Autumn 1889 an inoffensive elderly gentleman was knocked down by such a gang, robbed, kicked about the head, and taken up insensible; he was carried home and died the next day.

Today, the death of Emma Smith has been set in history as the first of the 'Whitechapel Murders' and although most historians would not put her murder down to Jack the Ripper there could be a possibility that the Ripper may have been part of the gang which assaulted her. It could also be possible that the attack awakened a stronger desire to carry out more intense mutilations, leading to one individual leaving the gang to fulfil his lone fantasies.

They say that serial killers 'find their feet', method-wise, before settling into specific behavioural patterns and the attack on a prostitute with the genitals being targeted would become a much more regular feature in the coming months. It's an intriguing possibility.

Although most researchers would discount the death of Emma Smith being the work of the Ripper, the same cannot be said about the next victim, Martha Tabram.

It's been fashionable since the late 1980's to refer to the Jack the Ripper victims as the canonical five, but this theory has come under increasing challenge in modern times. We have become familiar with behavioural traits of serial killers; we can see that the more they kill the more they develop – and alter- their methods of killing to suit their needs and reduce the risk of capture. Today we are more impressed by "signature" factors – the motivation for the crimes – than just simple modus operandi. Serial killers often vary their MO from crime to crime but their signature remains the same.

The atmospheric Gunthorpe Street still conjures up the public perception of Jack the Ripper's London.

Gunthorpe Street looking towards Whitechapel High St in 2021.

When you apply this to the Ripper case then the murder of Martha Tabram should almost certainly be included as Jack the Ripper murder. This particular murder was committed just 3 weeks before that of Mary Ann Nichols, the first of the canonical five.

The mutilated body of 39-year-old Martha Tabram was discovered laying on the landing of George Yard Buildings on 7 August 1888.

However, what set this murder apart from other tragic cases in the area was this was not just another attack on a vulnerable prostitute. Instead, this was a vicious, unprovoked attack on a defenceless victim. Tabram's body was peppered with 39 separate stab wounds. Many of her vital organs had been punctured and a decisive wound to her breastbone had apparently been delivered by a large dagger or bayonet. A murder as brutal as this completely shocked the police and the East End community alike. On the streets of the East End, the death of Emma Smith the previous April was still a very recent memory. Similarly, the fact that her attack took place only a few hundred yards from where Martha Tabram's body was found flagged up a frightening possibility that the two were connected.

The press noted the increased savagery of the murder, adding that, "the circumstances of this awful tragedy are not only surrounded with the deepest mystery, but there is also a feeling of insecurity to think that in a great city like London, the streets of which are continually patrolled by police, a woman could be so vilely and horribly killed – almost next to the citizens peacefully sleeping in their beds..."

Born in 1849, Martha Tabram was an East End prostitute living in a dosshouse in nearby George Street. Her marriage, which produced two children, fell apart in 1875 due to problems associated with her excessive drinking. Since then, she had been earning a living through prostitution and street-hawking, the latter with her new partner, Henry Turner.

On the last night of Martha Tabram's life, drink played an important part. According to her companion that evening, a notorious prostitute named Mary Ann Connolly (or 'Pearly Poll'), the pair had been drinking in a number of pubs in the area and had picked up two soldiers, a Private and a Corporal.

After several drinks in several establishments, Martha Tabram and Pearly Poll parted ways at 11.45pm. Connolly went up to Angel Alley with the Corporal, whereas Tabram ventured up to George Yard with the Private, undoubtedly for sex.

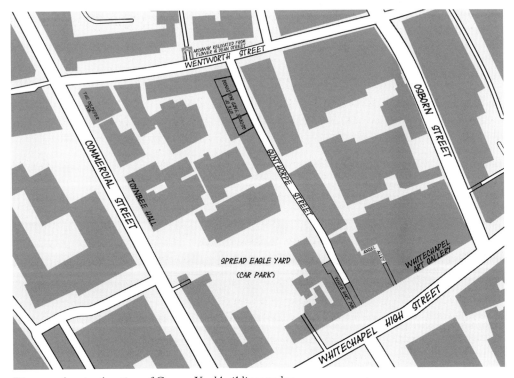

Diagram showing location of George Yard buildings today.

At 2am, a young police officer named Thomas Barrett approached a loitering soldier at the top of George Yard. After hearing that the soldier was, "waiting for a chum who went off with a girl," Barrett moved him on. Several hours later, at 4.45am, John Reeves, a resident of George Yard Buildings, found Tabram's mutilated body lying in a pool of blood on the first-floor landing of the tenement.

It was clear that this fateful night had not been a peaceful one. A number of residents of the building spoke of an unsettled evening. Reeves and his wife had been awoken in the night by several disturbances in nearby Wentworth Street. Similarly, Francis Hewitt had heard a shout of 'murder' coming from the street outside.

Returning from work at about 3.30am, Alfred Crow passed a figure lying on the first-floor landing. However, he was used to seeing people sleeping rough in the tenement's stairwell and he paid no heed. The figure was probably Martha Tabram's body.

For Scotland Yard, the murder investigation immediately focused on finding the identity of the soldiers that the two women had been seen with on the night of the murder, as well as identifying the man who was seen by PC Barrett.

After a lot of trouble, Mary Ann Connolly was traced and put before a line-up of soldiers who had been off duty on the night of the 7 August. Two ID parades took

A modern apartment block, in the grounds of Toynbee hall, now sits on the site where Martha Tabram was found murdered.

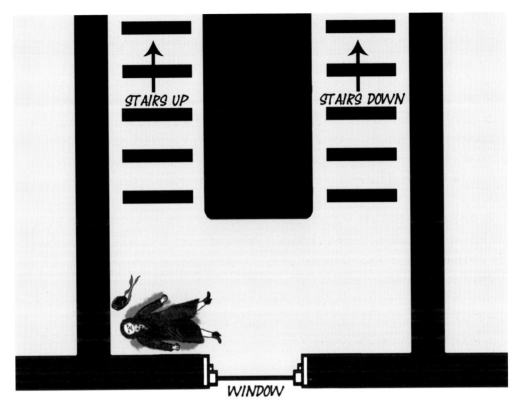

Crime scene diagram showing how Martha Tabram's body lay on the first floor landing.

place. In one, Connolly claimed that the soldiers were not present. In the second, she picked out two men who had impeccable alibis. PC Barrett also attended an ID parade. Again, he picked out men who could account for their movements on that fateful night. No conclusive findings arose from the ID parades and effectively the murder investigation ground to a halt.

Martha Tabram's body was formally identified on 14 August 1888, by her estranged husband Henry, of 6 River Terrace, East Greenwich. Unfortunately this was only done after her burial and her mortuary photograph was probably the only means by which identification could be made. But because her id took place after burial, sadly her burial register to this day simply says "unknown woman".

One of the most interesting aspects in the Tabram murder is that the doctor who examined her body gave his opinion that two weapons had been used in the attack. Dr Timothy Killean decided that one of the injuries was apparently caused by a bayonet or a dagger, ie a double bladed knife. (These would not necessarily have to have belonged to anyone with a military background because they were openly being sold in the markets less than 400 yards from the murder site) This is highly questionable; modern forensic medicine has pointed out that it is often possible to mistake a single bladed knife for a double bladed one, especially when the former is used with great force. It's also worth pointing out Killeen was not a police surgeon and had only been qualified for three years. Secondly, he had already heard from police and witnesses that Tabram was last seen in company of a soldier. His findings were more than likely influenced by such information and the real possibility that this soldier may be charged with her murder.

So, was Martha Tabram the First Jack the Ripper Victim?

Some researchers feel that because her throat had not been cut open or that there was no mutilation of the abdomen that she must have been a victim of another killer. Martha Tabram's wound patterns were distinctly different from the later Canonical Five murders, in that she received only multiple stab wounds as opposed to being slashed open or disembowelled, which is believed to be the modus operandi of the Ripper.

Yet there are circumstances of the crime that point very clearly to Jack the Ripper.

A resident of George Yard buildings discovering the body on 7 August 1888.

1. The victim was a prostitute
2. A knife was used in the attack
3. The body had been positioned. It lay on its back, legs apart and the clothes had been pushed up.
4. The victim had been murdered in the early hours of the morning
5. The location of the crime was in the centre of the Jack the Ripper killing territory.
6. The killer targeted the throat, abdomen and groin area (this latter injury was an incision three inches long, one inch deep, delicately described at the inquest as to the "lower portion of her body") From the similarity in the Ripper case it is clear that the murderer not only targeted the throat and abdomen, but also gained his satisfaction from attacking his victims' genitalia, a common trait in sexually motivated murder.

None of Tabram's wounds would have been immediately fatal, so no doubt the killer was covered in blood spurt. The killer would have learned from this and thus when we see the next murder (the first of the Jack the Ripper murders) we see signs of strangulation, followed by the throat being cut. Once this was done, there would be no more blood spurt.

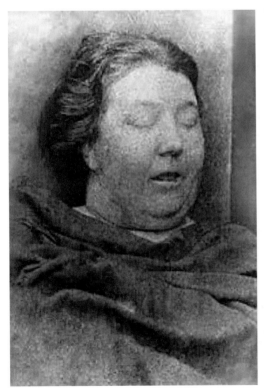

Martha Tabram mortuary photograph.

If we went back to 1888, Martha Tabram would be considered the first potential victim of the Whitechapel murderer for many years, by the actual officers involved in the case. This was a school of thought that would carry on almost unopposed until the mid-20th century. It is the opinion of this author that the police got it right the first time around and Martha Tabram should, once again, be considered the first Ripper victim.

Re-visiting the murder site today we can see, George Yard has changed to Gunthorpe Street; this was done in 1912 and named after the 13th century rector of the original St Mary's Whitechapel church, John Gunthorpe. Incredibly over 130 years later the cobbled Gunthorpe Street, more than any other location, still evokes the grime of 1888 Whitechapel, particularly when viewed from the narrow entrance on Whitechapel High Street. It should be noted that The White Hart pub still stands next to this entrance very much as it did back in 1888. It remains a favourite spot for locals, students and tour guides to all hang out after work and to this day remains the only pub in London with Ripper memorabilia on the walls. Its link to Jack rests with a barber called George Chapman who occupied a shop that once stood in the pub's basement. Chapman was a known killer and a favourite suspect of Inspector Abberline.

At the opposite end of Gunthorpe Street, the building where Martha Tabram's body was discovered was demolished in 1972 to make way for the nearby Toynbee Hall to be extended, but not before the writer Winston Ramsey managed to save the front gates that led through the gothic archway. It's now a lovely garden feature at his home.

George Yard Buildings were eventually taken over by Toynbee Hall as residences and offices a few years after the murder and were ultimately demolished in the 1970's and replaced by the modern Sunley House, which served the same purpose. A few years ago, Sunley House was itself demolished to make way for a new residential development which, when completed, will also front onto Wentworth Street named London Square. Interestingly, a small piece of College Buildings, erected in the 1880's, still stands on Wentworth Street and is being incorporated into the new project.

Even amongst the hustle and bustle of modern London life, this dingy back alley still conjures up images of the darkest days of the East End slums, especially when viewed from the White Hart pub located at the Whitechapel High Street entrance. On any given night you will see scores of tourists taking part in Jack the Ripper tours descending upon this particular area.

Chapter 2

Mary Ann Nichols

"…there is a woman lying on the pavement…
…I believe she is dead!"

Charles Cross

Durward Street didn't always go by this name; at the time of the Jack the Ripper murders it was known as Bucks Row, which could have been a slight variation of its former name 'Ducking Pond Row'. It would seem that back in the early days this was the location of a real ducking pond. Some East End historians believe it became locally known as Duck's Row then as the years moved on it changed to Bucks Row.

Bucks Row ran from Brady Street to Thomas Street, then the rest of the street ran from Whites Row to Bakers Row (The latter now called Vallance Road, and more infamous as the home of gangsters Ronnie and Reggie Kray). The north side

Bucks Row.

PC John Neil discovering the body of Mary Ann Nichols on 31 August 1888.

of the street had a row of large warehouses belonging to Brown and Eagle, to the west of this stood Essex Wharf.

On the south side and the corner of Brady Street stood The Roebuck pub and from there ran a line of terrace cottages. These had appeared in the early nineteenth century, between 1865 and 1872. They were basic two up two down houses. These little houses were ideal for the industrial workers of the age and despite the reputation of the area the street was regarded as quite respectable.

Bucks Row was about 20 feet wide and had a small 3 feet wide pavement that ran alongside the houses. At the end of these houses you would have a break in the pavement and here you would have seen two large wooden gates around 9 feet high which marked the entrance to Browns stable yard, after this there was a long brick wall behind which lay the train tracks of the East London Railway, and at the end of this wall you would then come to a large board school which had been constructed in 1876/77 and stood on the site of an earlier ragged school which was built in 1862.

It was here in the pre-dawn darkness hours of 31 August 1888, that Cart (Carman) driver Charles Cross of 22 Doveton Street, Bethnal Green, discovered the body of 43 year old Mary Ann Nichols.

Cross had been making his way to work along Bucks Row around 3.40am when he noticed something lying in the gap of the pavement, by the gateway of Browns

Stable yard. He decided to stop and investigate. At first glance, he thought that it might be a piece of discarded tarpaulin. As he stood there in the dark he realised that the "tarpaulin" was in fact the body of a woman lying on her back, her feet pointing towards the board school and her head pointed towards the cottages. Her bonnet was lying on the ground close to her left hand which was touching the gate. Both gates were closed.

He was soon joined by another passer-by, Robert Paul, also a carman, who lived at 30 Foster Street, Bethnal Green. Both men now stood over the body and tried their best to determine whether she was drunk, injured or dead. When they touched the woman's face they found it warm, but her hands were limp and cold. Her skirts had been raised, possibly exposing her genitals, so they might have assumed that she had been raped, but it was so dark that they could not see any further injuries, nor could they ascertain whether she was still alive. The gas lamps on the streets of Whitechapel were more used for guidance than actually illuminating the area and with each lamp giving out around five feet of light it's really no wonder the two men couldn't notice any other details.

They also had another issue. Both men were running late for work. Paul and Cross pulled down the woman's skirt to her knees in an attempt to preserve her decency and set off down the street, agreeing to alert the first policeman they came across, which they did when they saw PC Jonas Mizen on his beat at the junction of Bakers Row and Hanbury Street.

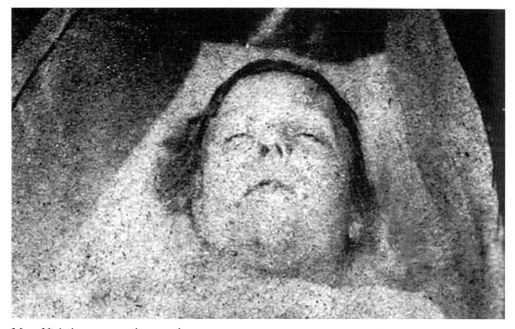

Mary Nichols mortuary photograph.

Had they waited a few minutes longer, they would have met PC John Neil as he came around the corner of Buck's Row. Neil was on his usual beat and had passed by the same spot some 30 minutes before. At that time, all had been well, there was nothing suspicious in the area. When he saw the body lying in the gateway, he too stopped to investigate. Unlike Cross and Paul, however, PC Neil had a bulls-eye lantern. He shone his light down upon the body, and saw a horrible sight.

The woman was clearly dead, with her eyes wide open and staring into the darkness. Blood oozed from two deep wounds in her throat, which had been slashed open all the way back to her spine.

Neil noticed a fellow officer nearby on Brady Street and immediately signalled for help. PC Thain came to his assistance and upon seeing the body went swiftly to fetch Dr Llewellyn, a local police physician. Dr Llewellyn's surgery was only around the corner at 152 Whitechapel Road. When Llewellyn arrived on the scene around 4.00 am he quickly declared the woman dead.

Woods Buildings 2021.

He examined the body, and found that her hands and arms were cold but her trunk and legs were warm, leading him to believe that the victim had been dead no more than half an hour. He ordered the body taken to the mortuary. This was done by loading the body onto a hand cart, covered with a blanket and then physically wheeled to a nearby mortuary for examination. The crime scene would then be quickly "processed" – which means it was washed clean of blood so as to avoid attracting unwelcome attention and unrest. It was an understandable course of action.

In 1888, forensic science was very much in its infancy. It was not possible to distinguish between human and animal blood, and it certainly wasn't possible to test other physical residues, -saliva, hair or sperm – at the scene of a crime. Fingerprints were also out of the question. The technique of fingerprinting was not used by Scotland Yard until 1901.

On-the-spot analysis largely consisted of looking for clues, such as something dropped by the murderer or finding an eye witness to the crime. The officers soon started knocking on doors and waking people up in the hopes that someone may have seen or heard the murder taking place. One such door was that of Essex Wharf. This building looked directly onto the murder site. Walter Purkiss and

Wood's Buildings, linking Whitechapel Road to Bucks Row. Did the Ripper escape through here?

his family resided here, his wife claimed to have been awake, other residents also claimed to have been light sleepers but nobody heard a thing. It would appear the killer had entered Bucks Row, committed his crime and fled without making a sound. Such actions would later add to the myth and legend of the Ripper story.

It should be noted that one of the myths surrounding this particular Jack the Ripper murder was that there were no easy escape routes from Buck's Row, but that depends on what you mean by easy. True, going East was difficult with just one road, but if one walked to the board school less than 50 yards to the west it was a very different story. You could go straight on west along Bucks Row of course, or you could head north or south via the various streets to the west of the school, including Court, Thomas, Queen Ann Streets or simply have taken Woods Buildings, a narrow alleyway (lovingly called piss ally) located behind the board school which ran directly onto Whitechapel Road. My own personal opinion is that Mary Nichols met her killer on the Whitechapel Road and took him to the board school via this alley and the killer simply doubled back after he was done.

But even if you don't believe this is what happened, there were in fact over 20 other possible variations on escape routes from the murder site.

The body of Mary Nichols was taken to the Whitechapel mortuary, just off today's Old Montague Street. The building was tiny, little more than a shed, and

The Working Lads institute on Whitechapel Road, where the inquest was held into several of the Ripper murders. Durward Street (formerly Bucks Row) lies just behind this building.

The former Frying Pan pub 2021.

once there, an examination was conducted by the duty inspector, John Spratling. Mortuary staff Robert Mann and James Hatfield stripped the body down at 6.30am and discovered something that Dr Llewellyn's initial examination had missed. The victim's stomach had been ripped open up to her sternum and her intestines were protruding through the gaping hole. She had been disembowelled.

Dr Llewellyn was called back to make a more thorough examination of the body. He noted a number of bruises on the victim's face and neck, probably caused by the murderer's gripping fingers and two fearsome cuts across the throat, one four inches and the other 8 inches long. The abdomen had been ripped in a deep jagged wound that ran downwards from left to right. He also noted several lacerations across the abdomen and three cuts or four cuts running downwards on the right side. There were also stab wounds in the vagina.

He would later state that the knife appeared to have been held in the left hand by a killer who had struck with strength and power, plunging the knife down in to the body as it lay prone on the ground. He would also speculate that the killer

The original pub sign can still be seen in the top brick work of the building.

must have possessed anatomical knowledge, knowing all the vital parts to attack. The attack itself would have lasted (in his opinion) 4 or 5 minutes, although death would have been instantaneous and most of the injuries would have been inflicted post mortem by the same knife – the only weapon used by the attacker.

Identification of the deceased came when her petticoat was found to carry the markings of Lambeth Workhouse. When inquiries were made, the victim was quickly identified as Mary Ann Nichols, nicknamed Polly, a 43-year-old prostitute. She had been married by the age of 18 to a man named William Nichols, a printer by trade. They had six children, but their marriage fell apart due to Polly's drinking. She had spent several years in Lambeth Workhouse and a few months as a servant before ending up in a doss house in Flower and Dean Street.

She was described as around 5ft 2inches in height with a dark complexion, brown eyes and hair (the latter turning grey) and had five front teeth missing. Despite this she was described as more youthful looking than her 43 years. She pretty much carried all she owned on the night she died. Her possessions amounted to a small piece of broken mirror, possibly the only way to properly see her reflection, a comb and small handkerchief. Friends described her as someone who kept herself clean and presentable.

The inquest into Polly Nichols' death opened at the Working Lads Institute at 137 Whitechapel Road. This building still exists and can be seen standing next to the entrance of Whitechapel Underground station, although it has now been converted into apartments. The Working Lads sign is still visible on the brick work.

It was here that several witnesses were questioned by the Coroner, Wayne Baxter, and with their testimony the final hours of Polly's life became clear.

According to the report filed by Inspector Joseph Helson (J Division), on the night of her death she was seen leaving the Frying Pan pub on Brick Lane at 12.30am on 31 August. Again, like the Working Lads Institute, this building has also survived the test of time and scores of modern tourists file past it on a nightly basis on several Jack the Ripper tours operating in the area.

Strangely nobody really knows (or can agree on) when the pub was actually built, but the western side of Brick Lane, where it sits, was built around the 1650's. We do know by 1888 the pub's landlord William Farrow, along with his brother Henry, ran several other pubs in the nearby area, including the Archers pub, now called "The Buxton". It was a very popular haunt for the prostitutes of the area, due largely to the close proximity of the common lodging houses situated directly behind. There were 233 common lodging houses in Whitechapel. Some tried to maintain reasonable standards, but most were filthy and infested with vermin.

Whitechapel Road 2021 – Mary Nichols made her way along this stretch of road on the night of her death, after being kicked out of the lodging house for having no money.

Durward Street 2021.

They accommodated around 8,500 people a night in crowded, mixed dormitories. Sometimes as many as 80 beds were crammed into one room.

Sanitation was poor or non-existent in the cramped and overcrowded houses. The public house was the only place of entertainment and relaxation, and alcohol the only palliative available to counter the drudgery of living.

When darkness fell the busy thoroughfares and narrow alleyways situated behind the pub here made ideal locations to provide trade to passers-by or customers from the pub.

The Frying Pan kept its Victorian features until 1966 when sadly its interior was completely refurbished to make way for the modern ale house. The pub finally closed its doors in 1991 and was transformed into an Indian Restaurant, The Sheraz, then it became The Shad restaurant and the Brick Lane Hotel.

I've stayed here many a time and eaten downstairs in the restaurant and the staff and owners have embraced the building's past links with the Ripper story. Sadly at the time of writing the premises has once again closed its doors but rumours

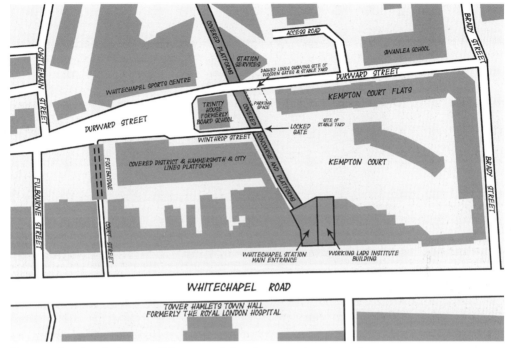

Diagram showing the lay out of the area and the crime scene location today.

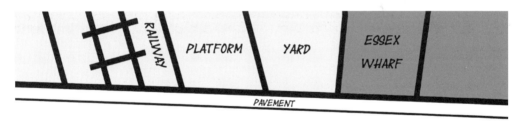

BUCK'S ROW

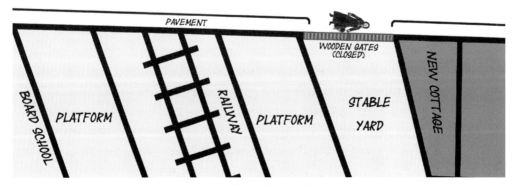

Crime scene image depicting how the body of Mary Ann Nichols was found.

Despite an uncertain future in the late 1980's, the Old Board School remained the only surviving building from 1888 on Bucks Row. It was eventually converted into apartments.

abound that the building could once again become a pub with the original Frying Pan name back in place. But for those modern travellers on the trail of Jack the Ripper, a nice glimpse into the past still remains by looking up to the top of the building and you can still see the original name – Ye frying pan – engraved into the terracotta.

When Mary Nichols was last seen here on the night of her death, she had made her lodging money several times during that day, but on each occasion she had spent it on gin. Drunk and broke, Polly returned to Wilmott's lodging house in nearby 18 Thrawl Street around 1.30am, but the lodge keeper turned her away. Like most doss houses, Polly's lodging house operated on a "no pay, no stay" basis. She told the deputy to keep the bed as she would soon get her doss money. "See what a jolly bonnet I've got", she cried to the deputy as she sauntered away, confident that her new hat (made of straw and of a better quality than the usual for one such as Polly) would quickly attract a client and the money she so desperately needed.

A final sighting of her took place on the junction of Osborn Street and Whitechapel Road, when a woman called Emily Holland spotted Mary leaning against a grocer's shop. This was around 2.30am and she was more than likely the worse for wear through drink. Having failed to convince her to return to the relative safety of the lodging house, Emily took a last glimpse of Mary as she headed in the direction of Whitechapel station.

The crime scene location today, next to the new entrance to Whitechapel Station and the former board school.

A marker near the spot where Mary Ann Nichols was buried in City of London Cemetery.

At some point in the next hour, Polly Nichols met a client and led him into the quiet seclusion of Buck's Row. That client was Jack the Ripper.

Mary Nichols was laid to rest on Thursday, 6 September, 1888 at City of London Cemetery. The funeral expenses were paid for by Edward Walker (Polly's father) and William Nichols (Polly's ex-husband). By the late 1990's the cemetery authorities decided to finally mark the area surrounding her grave site with a plaque.

When you visit the crime scene today you will see Buck's Row is now a noisy and busy construction site as part of the new Crossrail project. It has changed massively with very little of the original street left. It was renamed Durward Street in 1892 in an attempt to shrug off the notoriety given to it by the murder. A charming little story as the postmen mockingly call it "Killer's row"

The cottages that lined the route were considered slum type dwellings by the 1960's and unfit for human habitation. One report stated "the unfit houses have defects including disrepair, dampness, insufficient natural lighting and ventilation, inconveniently situated sanitary accommodation and inadequate facilities for the storage and preparation of food ". It wasn't long after that plans were made to demolish the lot. By September 1971 all tenants were removed from the houses and re-located elsewhere, the wrecking ball came in and by January 1972 they had ceased to exist.

Most of the warehousing on the northern part of Buck's Row had been demolished by 1970 and the rest, including Essex Wharf where Walter Purkis and his family lived (and directly opposite the murder site) had all come down by 1990. By 1995 The Roebuck pub was also demolished. The area would lie vacant for the best part of a decade before a new school, Swanlea, was constructed on the north side and new residential blocks appeared to the south soon after. Unfortunately now today, no real evidence of the original street exists.

Except for one sole survivor.

The only landmark remaining from 1888 is the old board school building, it's still a dominant building on the street and is one of the last sites that would have been seen by Mary Nichols on the night of her death. The fact that this building has survived has been quite incredible. It closed its doors in 1911, survived the second world war and the massive slum clearance of the 1970's and even numerous fires and vandalism that took place throughout the 1980's, which seemed certain to finally doom the building.

Luckily By 1996 the board school had been saved from the wrecking ball and converted into nice apartments and renamed Trinity Hall. Although everything in the street has changed in the last 130 years, and even with plenty of construction going on with the new Whitechapel overground station being built you can still go there as darkness falls and gaze up at the looming school house, and for the briefest of seconds, you could once again be back in 1888.

Chapter 3

Annie Chapman

"The ghoul-like creature who stalks the streets of London is simply drunk with blood, and he will have more."

The Star – 8 September, 1888

The Ripper's next victim was discovered in the back yard of number 29 Hanbury Street in the early hours of 8 September 1888, a mere seven days following the murder of Mary Ann Nichols. But modern visitors to Hanbury Street will be disappointed that nothing of number 29 (or indeed the whole block) stands there anymore, except a large extension to the Old Trueman brewery. But luckily you only have to turn 180 degrees and observe the houses on the other side of the street to give you the exact building construction which would

Looking down Brick Lane towards the Old Trueman brewery from the corner of Hanbury Street 2021.

Looking up Commercial Street. The Golden Heart pub sits on the corner of Hanbury Street.

have been used for number 29. The opposite side of the street has kept some of its original three storey houses that were built by the French Huguenots around the 1780's and the interiors are almost identical to that of number 29. If you pass by some dark night and see a door slightly open I encourage a sneak peek through, you will be looking at practically the same layout as the original crime scene.

Transporting you back to 1888, and to number 29 Hanbury Street, the shop on the ground floor was run by a Mrs Harriet Hardiman and was a cat meat shop. A single door led into the building. Once you walked in, a narrow hallway lay before you, roughly 20 feet in length and around 10 feet wide. At the end of the hallway was a staircase which led upstairs to the residents' accommodation. To the right of the stairs was another passageway that led to the back yard door. This door was generally left unlocked and once opened you could descend two stone steps and into a 14 feet square paved rear yard. Each yard was divided up by wooden fences measuring about 5 feet in height. An outside toilet lay at the rear of the yard to the right and to the left there was a work shed. These dark hallways and yards would no doubt be an ideal area for the occasional homeless person to sleep the night away or for prostitutes to service their clients away from prying eyes.

Number 29 Hanbury Street.

   The building housed 17 residents, spread across just eight small rooms. One room alone was occupied by a family of five adults. One of those residents, John Davis, had woken around 5.45am for work and on his way down the stairs he noticed the front door lying open. He then proceeded to go to the back door, which was closed,

The location of number 29 Hanbury Street today.

and pushed it open. He glanced down and in the gap between the two stone steps and the fence he found the mutilated remains of 47 year old Annie Chapman, her head by the steps and her feet pointing to the rear of the yard. "I saw a female lying down" he would later explain, "her clothing up to her knees, and her face covered in blood. What was lying beside her I cannot describe – it was part of her body"

Upon seeing the frightful sight, Davis ran out on to Hanbury Street and summoned help. It was 6am, dawn had broken and police quickly converged on the yard, as did crowds of onlookers.

The victim turned out to be another East End unfortunate, who had been living with around 114 other homeless at Crossingham's lodging house in Dorset Street at the time of her death. Annie Chapman was like many other women who walked the streets of Whitechapel after dark. At 47 years of age, she was in failing health. Years of alcohol abuse and hard living had left her with chronic lung disease and inflamed membranes of the brain. Her stout 5 foot frame hid the damage done by

The rear yard of 29 Hanbury Street where the body of Annie Chapman was discovered.

decades of alcoholism, a habit she supported with prostitution. The evidence we have clearly suggests she would have soon been dead in any case.

By the time of her fateful meeting with her murderer, Annie Chapman, known as Dark Annie to her friends, had fallen down to the deepest, darkest depths of Victorian society. In 1869, she had married a coachman named John Chapman. They moved around London before settling in Windsor and had eight children, but the marriage was fraught with problems and tragedy. Of their eight children, the eldest daughter had died of meningitis at a young age and the youngest, a boy, was a cripple.

Annie turned to alcohol and in return this took a heavy toll on the marriage which eventually ended in 1884. However, her husband continued to provide financial assistance in the shape of ten shillings a week after the separation for her to get by. Following his death in 1886, the money dried up, pushing Annie to Spitalfields, where lodgings were cheap and easy to come by. She tried selling crocheted flowers to earn a meagre living, but of course, when times were hard, she would earn her living on the streets. Her fall from grace is evident in that she remains the only known victim of Jack the Ripper to have been photographed in life. A luxury none of the other victims could afford.

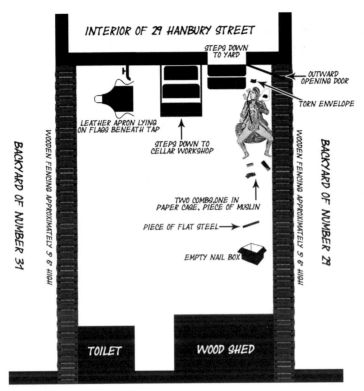

On the evening of 7 September, Annie Chapman, like Polly Nichols, found herself without the four pence necessary to buy her evening's lodgings. Already drunk and completely broke, Annie Chapman was last seen stumbling away from her lodging house in Dorset Street by a deputy. She walked through to Brushfield Street and then up towards Christ Church Spitalfields and eventually Hanbury Street.

Around 5.30 am, Mrs Elizabeth Long claimed she was hurrying through the pre-dawn light on an early morning errand. She was sure of the time because she had heard the Trueman Brewery clock chime. Historians have suggested she was probably mistaken and it was in fact the 5.15am chime.

She turned from Brick Lane on to Hanbury Street, where she noticed a man and a woman standing in the doorway of Number 29. She would later identify the woman as Annie Chapman. The man had his back to Mrs Long, but as she passed, she heard the man ask, "Will you?" The woman replied, "Yes." She noticed that the man was taller than the woman, that he wore a long, dark coat and a brown deerstalker hat, and that his look was that of a foreigner with a shabby but genteel appearance.

The body of Annie Chapman was in a horrendous state and shocked all who had the grave misfortune of seeing it. She was lying on her back with her legs drawn up, the feet resting on the ground with her knees spread outwards and her face covered in blood. The offender of a sexual homicide often leaves his victims in a degrading position; Martha Tabram, Mary Ann Nichols and now Annie Chapman had all been found with their legs apart and clothing pulled up to expose them. These are the acts that a killer must perform to fulfil his fantasy and complete the act he has imagined in his head. And as these acts are repeated again they are now his signature factors.

Her head was turned to the right, fresh bruising was evident on the chin and sides of the jaw. Her face and tongue were swollen, the tongue protruding through her teeth heavily

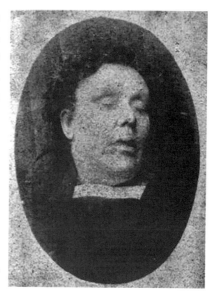

Annie Chapman mortuary photograph.

suggesting she had been choked to death first. Further evidence of this is in the fact her face, lips and hands were black and blue (as when breathing has stopped), rather than white (as through loss of blood).

She had blood stained hands, one of them was lying up close to her chest suggesting the poor woman had probably fought for her life and being a heavier set woman than the others the killer may have struggled to overpower or throttle her. Sadly we will never know.

Her throat had then been cut twice from left to right with such force and depth that she was nearly decapitated. The muscles of her neck had been separated, suggesting that the killer had sawn at the wound to get it right down to the bone, raising the possibility that he did indeed intend to remove her head.

Her dress had been lifted to expose her red and white striped stockings. Her abdomen had been ripped open, with her small intestine lifted out and placed by her right shoulder. The blood on her face may suggest the killer threw the intestines into her face first and it then slid off onto the ground. By her left shoulder lay two other portions of her abdominal organs. Her womb, upper vagina and much of her bladder were missing from the crime scene, suggesting that the killer had probably taken them with him.

Dr Phillips arrived on the scene at 6.30am, he estimated Annie Chapman's time of death to be two or three hours previously. However, later accounts note that the chill of the morning and the extensive loss of blood might have made it difficult for the doctor to get an accurate time, particularly since he did not use a thermometer but relied on touch. Dr Phillips also noticed an oddity about the scene. Two rings

GHASTLY
MURDER
IN THE EAST-END.
DREADFUL MUTILATION OF A WOMAN.

Capture : Leather Apron

Another murder of a character even more diabolical than that perpetrated in Buck's Row, on Friday week, was discovered in the same neighbourhood, on Saturday morning. At about six o'clock a woman was found lying in a back yard at the foot of a passage leading to a lodging-house in a Old Brown's Lane, Spitalfields. The house is occupied by a Mrs. Richardson, who lets it out to lodgers, and the door which admits to this passage, at the foot of which lies the yard where the body was found, is always open for the convenience of lodgers. A lodger named Davis was going down to work at the time mentioned and found the woman lying on her back close to the flight of steps leading into the yard. Her throat was cut in a fearful manner. The woman's body had been completely ripped open, and the heart and other organs laying about the place, and portions of the entrails round the victim's neck. An excited crowd gathered in front of Mrs. Richardson's house and also round the mortuary in old Montague Street, whither the body was quickly conveyed. As the body lies in the rough coffin in which it has been placed in the mortuary —the same coffin in which the unfortunate Mrs. Nicholls was first placed—it presents a fearful sight. The body is that of a woman about 45 years of age. The height is exactly five feet. The complexion is fair, with wavy dark brown hair; the eyes are blue, and two lower teeth have been knocked out. The nose is rather large and prominent.

Police posters issued around the East End at the time giving the killers nickname 'Leather Apron'.

appeared to have been wrenched from her fingers and taken away. Also her belongings, including a small piece of coarse muslin, a toothed comb, a torn piece of envelope and two pills had all been removed from the body and arranged around her feet. Speculation on this arrangement continues to rage – was this done by the killer? If so, why?

Dr Phillips conducted a more detailed examination of the body, seeking details that would assist the police. He later stated, "Obviously the work was that of an expert or one, at least, who had such knowledge of anatomical or pathological examinations as to be able to secure the pelvic organs with one sweep of the knife."

The Knife was estimated to be around 6 inches in length. This suggested it could be the same knife as used by doctors but it was also noted that a slaughterman's knife would also be possible. The opinion that the murder weapon was not an ordinary knife, but perhaps an amputating knife, has led to the idea that the Ripper may have had medical training. Speculation regarding practicing medical personnel and students raged at the time and still impacts investigations into the identity of the murderer.

Statements were taken from those living on Hanbury Street. One man, a carpenter called Albert Cadosch, told police that he had entered the back yard of his residence at Number 27 around 5.25 am to use the lavatory. He heard a woman's voice cry "No!". Three minutes later he returned to the yard again only to hear a thud noise almost like something had fallen against the fence separating his yard from Number 29. Was this Annie Chapman in a final struggle with her assailant?

The fence was only five feet high, and had he looked over it, Albert Cadosch might have actually seen Jack the Ripper and history would be very different. However, life in Hanbury Street had clearly taught Mr Cadosch to keep a low profile, and he hurried off to work along Commercial Street, marking the time on the clock of Spitalfields Church as he passed. It was 5.32 am.

By now there was an intense crowd numbering several hundred gathering on the street outside. Some of the more enterprising residents of the houses surrounding

The Trueman Brewery. Elizabeth Long claimed to have heard the clock chiming around 5.30am the morning of the murder.

29 Hanbury Street quickly realised that the onlookers were desperate for a glimpse into the bloody drama which had unfolded around them and allowed people to pay to get into the buildings, where they could look out the back windows on to the gory yard where Annie Chapman's body was discovered.

But it was a surprise discovery that would whip the already excitable crowd into a frenzy. A brown leather apron was found in the yard. But why would this be? Was this a clue to the killer's identity?

Prior to the murder, the press had speculated that a Jewish man in the area, who was known to local prostitutes as "Leather Apron" might be responsible for the killings. He had harassed women before and was described as aggressive. Dubbed a semi mythical figure who terrorised prostitutes, the press had pointed fingers at the Jewish community several times, and many believed that the gruesome nature of the killings pointed to a foreigner rather than an Englishman.

While the leather apron found at Hanbury Street was eventually found to belong to a resident, one John Richardson, who had nothing to do with Annie Chapman's death, the people of Whitechapel were already primed to blame the Jews for the murders. The word on the streets was 'Leather Apron' and woe betide any man, particularly if they were foreign, who aroused the slightest suspicion, for within a short time they would find themselves being chased by lynch mobs, some of which were reported as being several hundred strong. Destruction of property and attacks on innocent Jewish men became all too common in the days following the murder. As the Press spurred the public into a panic with tantalising headlines and provocative stories, pressure mounted to provide the identity of the elusive killer.

The police found themselves simply overwhelmed with the heavy burden of not only following up medical students with a history of insanity or interviewing hundreds of local slaughtermen – both classes of person reckoned to have the necessary skill and knowledge for the mutilations they also had the extra burden of keeping the local people under control. Over two hundred lodging houses were checked within a mile of the murder site. None of the deputies or night watchmen questioned had any memory of any person stained with blood entering their premises, however they admitted that little attention is given to persons inquiring after a bed in the early hours of the morning. Persons entering the doss house are asked for their money and then led through a badly lit stairway to their room. The men in these houses use a common washing place and water, once used, is thrown down the sink by the lodger using it.

Despite their problems, the police did have a breakthrough on 10 September when the highly experienced Detective Sergeant William Thick arrested John Pizer at his home in Mulberry Street, Whitechapel. Sergeant Thick had known Pizer well for eighteen years and was convinced that he and 'Leather Apron' were one and the same. Unfortunately, as posters were going up proclaiming 'Arrest of Leather Apron', Pizer was released, after extensive questioning revealed that he had cast-iron alibis for the relevant nights and excellent witnesses to back him up. Despite fitting many of the criteria of 'Leather Apron', Pizer was innocent of the Whitechapel murders, something which must have been a disaster for the Metropolitan Police investigation.

Public hysteria now began to take over London. This spilled over into the West End. At the time the Lyceum theatre was presenting Dr Jekyll and Mr Hyde starring the American actor Richard Mansfield. The tale of a monster doctor terrorising the streets was almost too much of a coincidence for some. They saw this as "inspiring" or "encouraging" the murderer, with some even suggesting that Mansfield himself was the killer and soon the play was closed down.

Even at the inquest into Annie Chapman's death, rumours of doctors were rife. The coroner, Wynne Baxter, put forward the notion that body parts were being sold to an American doctor for study and research. The national press seized on the

Actor James Mason visits the murder site in the 1968 documentary, 'The London nobody knows'. Number 29 was demolished shortly afterwards.

suggestion with great enthusiasm, but the theory was rapidly mocked and scotched by the medical journals. Theories, gossip, stories and rumours engulfed the whole investigation.

By now the curiosity had even attracted the attention of West End thrill seekers who arrived and offered money to the locals to be taken around to the other murder sites, a practice which has continued to this day. These acts of enterprise and more were met with mixed emotions and those exploiting the murders for financial gain would often find themselves under attack by the locals.

The Irish Times 11 September noted:

"There is a waxworks show to which admission can be obtained for one penny, in the Whitechapel Road, near the Working Lad's Institute. During the past few days a highly coloured representation of the George Yard and Buck's Row murders – painted on canvas – have been hung in front of the buildings, in addition to which there were placards notifying that life size wax models could be seen within. The pictures have caused large crowds to assemble on the pavement in front of the shop. This morning, however, another picture was added to the rest. It was a representation of the murder in Hanbury Street. The prominent feature of the picture was that they were plentifully besmeared with red paint – this of course representing wounds and blood. Notices were posted up that a life-sized waxwork figure of Annie Chapman could be seen within. After the inquest at the Working Lads Institute had been adjourned, a large crowd seized them and tore them down. Considerable confusion followed, and order was only restored by the appearance of an Inspector of police and two Constables. A man attired in workman's clothes and who appeared to be somewhat the worse for drink then addressed the crowd. He said – "I suppose you are all Englishmen and women here; then do you think the picture (continued the orator, pointing to the one representing the murder in Hanbury Street) should be exhibited in the public streets before the poor woman's body is hardly cold." Cries of "no, no, we don't" greeted his remarks and another scene of excitement followed. The crowd however was quickly dispersed by the police before the showman's property was further damaged."

The East End of London with its maze of tightly-packed courts and alleyways had always been known as a dangerous place, roamed by gangs of thieves who would not hesitate to strike even in broad daylight. But the ferocious, sexual nature of these crimes shocked even the usually unshockable Whitechapel inhabitants. The East London observer reported "as darkness falls the streets are empty. By midnight, only a few brave souls and police remain on the streets". Whitechapel and Spitalfields was rarely quiet at night. Public houses and shops stayed open well past midnight and many opened again at dawn. It was truly a reign of terror unprecedented in the history of East London. The panic would hit the local businesses hard and this would eventually lead to the formation of early neighbourhood watch/vigilante groups, patrolling the area.

On 16 September the News of the World reported:

"A number of tradesmen in the neighbourhood in which the murder was committed have organised a vigilance committee, and the following notice is published: 'Finding that, in spite of murders being committed in our midst, our police force is inadequate to discover the author or authors of the late atrocities, we the undersigned, have formed ourselves into a committee and intend offering a substantial reward to anyone, citizen or otherwise, who shall give such information as will be the means of bringing the murderers to justice.'"

Annie Chapman's memorial marker sits in the area where her body was buried in Manor cemetery, London.

The Vigilance Committee and its chairman, George Lusk, were highly critical of the police and cited several recent street brawls in the area which had lasted for up to half an hour before a policeman arrived on the scene. The police had, in fact, drafted extra men into the area, many in plain clothes and some in disguise. The police presence was particularly heavy at weekends, as it was noted that this was when the killer struck. Such efforts did little to quell public criticism.

"The Detective Department at Scotland Yard is in an utterly hopeless and worthless condition," reported one East London newspaper. There were public meetings at which it was unanimously voted that the Home Secretary, Henry Matthews, and the Commissioner of Police, Sir Charles Warren, should resign.

Sir Charles Warren got the brunt of the public outrage, usually caricatured in the press as a crusty old soldier – he was 48 at the time of the murders – or a martinet concerned more with the imposition of military standards of discipline and organization than he was with combatting crime. The fact that he had been appointed for precisely that purpose is often ignored.

Warren had been recalled from his military duties in Sudan in 1886 when a crisis of public confidence in the effectiveness of the police had brought about the resignation of the previous Commissioner, Sir Edmund Henderson.

Despite his personality clashes with James Monro, the head of the CID, and with Henry Matthews, the Home Secretary, he had some success in reorganizing the force by 1888, just before the Ripper murders began. Monro resigned. His replacement, Robert Anderson, was appointed the day after the Mary Ann Nichols murder and did not return to London from holiday until after the double killing on 30 September. Heading the CID inquiry in his absence was Detective Chief Inspector Donald Swanson, with Detective Inspector Frederick Abberline in charge of the investigating team on the ground. These were the men now faced with bringing the Whitechapel murderer to justice.

Politically, the horrific murder of Annie Chapman was also considered an ideal opportunity for the radical press to draw attention to the grim conditions in East London and suddenly the murders were being used as a stick to beat the authorities with as radical, outspoken newspaper editorials laid into the police, particularly commissioner Sir Charles Warren, for their apparent incompetence. It was almost like overnight Annie Chapman had become almost a figurehead representing the plight of the poor in the East End:

"Dark Annie's spirit still walks Whitechapel, unavenged by Justice... And yet even this forlorn and despised citizeness of London cannot be said to have suffered in vain. "Dark Annie's" dreadful end has compelled a hundred thousand Londoners to reflect what it must be like to have no home at all except the "common kitchen" of a low lodging-house; to sit there, sick and weak and bruised and wretched, for lack of fourpence with which to pay for the right of a "doss"; to be turned out after midnight to earn the requisite pence, anywhere and anyhow; and in course of earning it to come across your murderer and to caress your assassin."

It might have been the reason why Annie Chapman was taken quietly and without public announcement from the mortuary at Old Montague Street on Friday, 14 September, 1888 and brought to Manor Park Cemetery for burial. Only the police, undertaker and few relatives knew of the arrangements. In a low key service she was buried at (public) grave 78, square 148. Sadly Chapman's grave no longer exists; it has since been buried over but a small plaque stands near the location area to this day.

As for 29 Hanbury Street, the downstairs shop went on to become a barber's shop in 1895, then it was taken over by Nathan Brill. It is his shop sign which features in most of the old images we have. I believe this sign stayed there right up until the end. In 1970, the site where Annie Chapman was murdered was finally demolished to make way for extensions to the Truman Brewery, which remains to this day. The area where Annie Chapman's body was discovered doubles as a car park for the surrounding brewery and on a Sunday plays host to a huge street food market. Interestingly, In recent years, following the brewery's closure, parts of the existing building were redeveloped into small shop units and although there is, once again, a 27 and 31 Hanbury Street, it was impossible to open up the relevant section where

29 once stood. However, this section has still been given a street number and a large 29 sits proudly in the spot where the infamous house used to be. It's a useful marker for those who wish to visit the exact location..

We have seen some memorable images of Hanbury Street taken over the years, which also includes the yard where the murder happened. Author and fellow ripperologist, the late great Colin Wilson, was lucky to have found his way into the back yard and was photographed alongside resident Kathleen Manning in the early 1960's giving many researchers their first glimpse of the crime scene.

But for those wishing to see what it really would have looked like, you are in luck. In 1967, the actor James Mason visited No.29 for a scene in the cult movie 'The London Nobody Knows' and in it he goes through the front door and through the passage into the yard to speak of the Ripper murders. The back yard was over grown and strewn with rubbish and broken pieces of discarded wood. It gives all the appearance of the slum it would have been in 1888. The sequence, which also includes other Spitalfields locations nearby, can be found on YouTube and is a fascinating snapshot of times past – and in colour!

Chapter 4

Ripper Land

"Welcome to the heart of Jack the Ripper's London"
Most often used quote by scores
of nightly Ripper tour guides

I have been conducting walking tours for many years in and around the back streets of Whitechapel and Spitalfields and the area I find the most fascinating is the journey one can take from Hanbury Street to Commercial Street, via Wilkes Street.

Brushfield Street.

The ever atmospheric Fournier Street, which runs between Commercial Street and Brick lane, is still lined with its original 18th century houses from the time of the Ripper murders.

Here you get a real ambience of bygone London and for a brief few minutes you can almost feel what it might have been like to walk the streets of the Victorian East End. Pretty much all around you are the original structures and areas from that time. Wilkes Street and Fournier Street are lined with houses from the 18th century. You have Puma Court which cuts through the buildings and is a perfect example of the dozens of little alleyways which aided the Ripper to come and go undetected.

As you walk around towards Commercial Street, you have the looming and almost sinister structure of Christ Church, built between 1714 and 1729 by the apprentice of Sir Christopher Wren and a prominent feature when gazed from the Brushfield Street end of the city of London. From here it looks almost like a gothic gate keeper to Spitalfields. It's hard to imagine this superb construction was once considered for demolition, due largely to the building falling into a bad state of disrepair back in the 1950's. Luckily the old lady was saved by a local charity

The looming figure of Christ Church on Commercial Street.

Christ Church and the Ten bells pub.

group and restored to her former glory. I think it is true to say no modern church in London has witnessed so many highs and lows, as much horror and degradation as this masterpiece. So I am glad that today she stands, immovable, imposing and immortal, over once again a vibrant area.

To the right of this is Itchy Park where the homeless would come to sleep during the day. Strangely enough it was illegal to sleep rough at night time in the East End. So when morning broke, lines of wretched souls would queue up to gain access to the church grounds and hopefully find a park bench or warm piece of grass to lay their head.

Opposite this would have been the entrance to Dorset Street, possibly the worst street in London at the time and so dangerous the police wouldn't venture down it unless they were in teams of four. It was here that the Ripper committed his most infamous and ghastly murder….. but I will return to this later.

To the right of where Dorset Street would have stood you have the famous Spitalfields market. The current building was rebuilt in 1887 and possibly posed a big problem back in 1888 when trying to find a killer armed with a knife. Hundreds of men, cart drivers, apprentices and market traders would be coming to and from the market along the busy commercial street, all probably armed with some kind of knife as a tool of their trade.

The famous Ten Bells Pub, once renamed 'The Jack the Ripper' back in the 1970's.

Interior of the Ten Bells. The bar has been placed back in the centre where it was originally in 1888.

All these structures would be visited at one time or another by the citizens of 1888. But probably none more so than The Ten Bells pub. There has been a public house on the site since at least the 1740s (possibly even before that, too!) and the establishment is still going strong today. When it first opened, the pub was actually called the Eight Bells pub, as it is named in keeping with the number of bells that Christ Church, opposite, had at the particular time.

I think it's safe to say that no journey into Ripperland can be complete without visiting the local drinking dens that would have been frequented by many of the Ripper's victims and I dare say Jack himself. When researching the case you find many of these pubs pop up in witness statements and articles of the day. There is a very good reason. Drink provided many with great, if only temporary, relief from the grim reality of the East End.

There were none of the licensing laws that we are used to today because many pubs stayed open well past midnight and some opened as early as 5am. Licence laws in the UK, as a modern society knows it, were only brought in during the war time years of the 1940's.

The original pub tile image titled, 'Spitalfields in ye Olden time'.

Now, as popular as the bars around Whitechapel were, it didn't mean everyone was a raging alcoholic. It's true that the victims of the Ripper had difficulties with drink, all were drunk the night they died, but the attraction of alcohol was sometimes to do with the lack of drinking water. The slums of the East End did not have running water that was clean enough for them to drink. Water was collected in rain barrels in yards or on street corners. If a barrel's lid was missing, the water would be polluted with dirt from passing traffic or dead rodents. Going for a glass of gin, therefore, might have been a more attractive alternative.

Out of all the pubs in the East End, it's the Ten Bells pub that has captured the imagination of the public the most. The pub stands at the corner of Commercial Street at the interchange with Fournier Street. It's almost as old as Nicholas Hawksmoor's mighty edifice of Christ Church, Spitalfields, which it sits beneath, almost like a parcel under a Christmas tree.

It is said that several of Jack's victims frequented the establishment before they were killed. In Spring 1888, Elizabeth Stride was thrown out of the pub for drunk and disorderly behaviour. Mary Jane Kelly was seen in the pub with a friend on the night before her death and allegedly, Annie Chapman was said to be drinking alone in the Ten Bells only hours before her body was later discovered.

The Crispin street refuge. From 1868 until 1931, thousands of homeless men and women would seek nightly shelter within the walls of this building. Today it houses student accommodation but still has the original signage above its doors.

Sandys Row. Some of these buildings, including the Jewish Synagogue (left), date back to 1766.

Artillery passage, Spitalfields.

Looking onto Wilkes Street from the corner of Princelet Street.

The pub has appeared in practically every major movie ever made on the case and appears in most graphic novels, stage plays and posters around the world. Often images show a lone woman standing by its doors and lurking in the shadows across the street is that top hat wearing phantom, ready to pounce.

The interior of the pub has kept its Victorian charm, sporting original tiles on the wall from the time of the Ripper, narrow staircases and dark corners, all this certainly adds to the atmosphere.

On 30 April 1975 – after a major refurb – the pub was renamed "Jack the Ripper" and new owner Bob Wayman transformed the venue into an afternoon strip tease bar for the nearby city workers. Scattered around its walls were memorabilia, posters, photographs and signage all relating to the Ripper case. A huge green and red "Jack the Ripper" board was placed in the corner of the room; this included a short description of the murders along with the names of the victims.

The pub did surprisingly well for its time and was no doubt a big hit with tourists and locals alike but by the start of the 1980's public opinion had started to turn.

One of the charming aspects of Wilkes street is the original houses, door frames, shutters and iron works still remain intact.

Almost 100 years since Jack walked the streets of London all the newspapers across the UK would be telling the story of another ripper operating in the North of England. Peter Sutcliffe aka The Yorkshire Ripper (as dubbed by the press due to the similarity with the original Jack) had terrorised the community for 5 years, killing 13 women and leaving 7 more for dead. In an almost re-enactment of the mass hysteria that had once gripped 1888, the new ripper murders would bring the same anger and protests.

Organised marches and women's rights groups took to the streets to highlight violence against women and it wasn't long before their attention would focus on the Jack the Ripper pub.

Kelly Ellenbourne from the protest group "women against violence against women said "it's outrageous that anyone should be using the historical and horrific murder of women as a tourist attraction to make money"

Eventually the protests died down but the seed of tastelessness had been planted in the minds of the public and soon the Brewery who owned the pub felt the time was right to get rid of the ghoulish pub name and all the memorabilia and revert to the more appropriate "Ten Bells"

By the turn of the century the only reference to the Ripper that remained on display in the pub was the three front covers of the police news that hung on the stairwell leading to the toilets. These too have since gone.

But, it isn't all Jack the Ripper. The pub is also famous for strange happenings and over the years staff and visitors alike have reported sightings of a range of ghostly apparitions in the pub. They include;

The Victorian Landlord

In the late 1990's, staff with rooms on the pub's upper floors frequently reported regular encounters with the ghost of a Victorian man. The staff would wake in the night feeling uneasy, turn over and see his ghostly form lying next to them! As soon as they called out, he would disappear.

Although the descriptions were always similar, nobody could pinpoint the man's identity. However, in 2000, a new landlord arrived. While clearing out the cellar, he found an old box hidden in a corner. The box contained items belonging to a

Looking up Fournier Street, towards Brick Lane.

To this day, Jack the Ripper tours still remain the most atmospheric and educational way of exploring 18th century Spitalfields.

certain George Roberts, including a wallet containing a 1900's press cutting talking about Roberts' murder. After further research, he found that Roberts had been the landlord of the pub around this time. Was it his ghost the staff kept seeing?

The Murdered Baby

Becoming aware of the ghostly activity, they called in a psychic to assess the building. All was fine until she got to the top floor of the pub, where she refused to enter a room. She declared that something terrible had taken place in the room, involving the death of a 19th-century baby.

Several years later, a researcher was touring the pub. While up in the roof space, she noticed some material behind the water tank. Upon further investigation, this turned out to be a sack containing a set of mouldy baby clothes dating back to the

Victorian era. Even more chillingly, the clothes looked to have been cut with a knife. The tank was located directly above the room the psychic had pointed out.

The Mysterious Poltergeist

In 2001, a tenant would often hear footsteps and laughter in the hallway outside his room, even when he was alone in the pub. Upon investigation, the corridor would always be empty. When heading down to the bar, he would sometimes be pushed by an invisible hand

Ghostly occurrences are still reported to this day.

By 2010, a new refurb had occurred in the Ten Bells, this time the designers made more of an effort to make sure that it stayed in keeping with the original style of décor employed at the time of the Ripper. Therefore, the bar was moved to the centre of the room, where it would have originally been back in 1888. Ghosts of the past resurfaced as the refurb team pulled down the front modern signage only to reveal the original 1888 "Trueman Beers" sign printed in gold capitals upon a deep green background. This now remains uncovered for all to see.

The original Victorian tiles on the surrounding walls have all been saved and it truly adds to the atmosphere when you realise that they are the same tiles that all the victims, locals, police and the Ripper himself once gazed at 133 years ago. One particular section of this stands out the most. A superb mosaic mural dating back to the late 1880's entitled "Spitalfields in ye olden times". The superb image depicts wealthy aristocrats coming to buy silks from a local weaver. What I did not know until very recently is that the tiled image was designed by William B Simpson and Sons, a company renowned for their tiled mosaic works across London at the time. The same company continues to maintain this image to this day.

The upper floors of the Ten Bells have now been reopened for the public and have dramatic views across the market, down Commercial Street and up to the spire of Christ Church, which looms overhead. I thoroughly recommend a visit anytime you find yourself in the area.

With so much to see from 1888 in this one little area alone it is hardly surprising to hear modern visitors state, "oh this is proper Ripper Land right here". I can't disagree.

Chapter 5

Dear Boss –

"Jack the Ripper? It's a newsman's dream!!"

Ben Bates – The Star

(TV series Jack the Ripper – 1988)

Today, in the public records office, written in blood red ink, remains probably the most infamous letter in the history of crime. Subject to fierce debate among historians and experts for over a century it is known as the "dear Boss letter." It was to alter the perception of the Whitechapel murders forever and created the most infamous nickname in history

It was received on 27 September 1888, almost three weeks following the death of Annie Chapman, at the Central News agency.

It read:

25th September 1888

Dear Boss,

I keep on hearing the police have caught me but they wont fix me just yet. I have laughed when they look so clever and talk about being on the right track. That joke about Leather Apron gave me real fits. I am down on whores and I shant quit ripping them till I do get buckled. Grand work the last job was. I gave the lady no time to squeal. How can they catch me now. I love my work and want to start again. You will soon hear of me with my funny little games. I saved some of the proper red stuff in a ginger beer bottle over the last job to write with but it went thick like glue and I cant use it. Red ink is fit enough I hope ha. ha. The next job I do I shall clip the ladys ears off and send to the police officers just for jolly wouldnt you. Keep this letter back till I do a bit more work, then give it out straight. My knife's so nice and sharp I want to get to work right away if I get a chance. Good Luck.

Yours truly

Jack the Ripper

Dont mind me giving the trade name

PS Wasnt good enough to post this before I got all the red ink off my hands curse it No luck yet. They say I'm a doctor now. Ha ha.

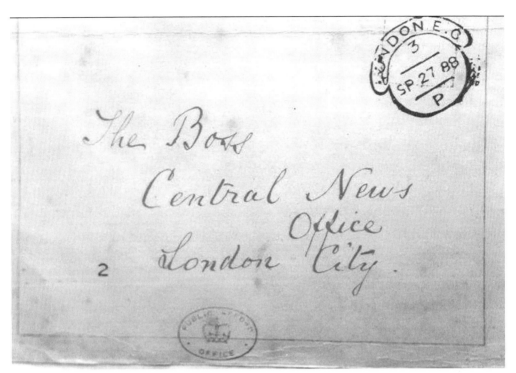

The envelope addressed to the Central News agency containing the 'Dear Boss' letter.

The agency did not release the text until 3 October, since it contained a prediction that no-one would have wanted to make public until it had been proved true or false. Some senior officers were convinced it was a hoax and modern historians have largely followed this conclusion.

Regardless who wrote the letter, the nickname was a fantastic piece of tabloid marketing, the name Jack the Ripper would become a news man's dream. Suddenly all of London had a name to go with the brutal killings and everything that was bad about the East End could be personified into one character.

It's true to say after a century the details of the crimes are forgotten by the outside world, but the name survives and when mentioned instantly conjures up images of Victorian nights and that shadowy figure lurking in the darkness, the eternal image of Jack the Ripper.

The press agency openly suggested that it was probably a joke, but nonetheless passed it on to the Metropolitan Police for further examination two days later. Although it is not clear how the police reacted initially, they followed the author's instructions and held the letter back until the murderer had done a 'bit more work' at which point (following the next murder) sections of the letter were reproduced in the press on 1 October. What caused the greatest impact, and indeed it is something that is still felt today, was the reproduction of the name 'Jack the Ripper', a perfect nickname for the as-yet-uncaught fiend of the East End.

The style of handwriting suggests an educated writer. Some believe the letter a hoax and possibly the words of a journalist.

Interestingly, this was not the first missive received by the authorities claiming to be written by the killer. Sir Charles Warren, Chief Commissioner of the Metropolitan Police, had been sent a rather rambling one a few days before but had given it no credence. It did not have a signature and was certainly not made public at the time, however the 'Dear Boss' letter, as it has become known, was guaranteed to cause a stir.

But was it genuine?

Much has been written about this most infamous of communications, the first of many that would be received by all and sundry for a long time to come. But as the first to be published and the first one to bear that now infamous name, it has become iconic. Whether the general public felt it was genuine is hard to say, but many of the leading police officers of the day – the men who had direct responsibility for the investigation of 1888 – were asked what they felt about it years later, and the general consensus was that it was a hoax from the pen of 'an enterprising London journalist.'

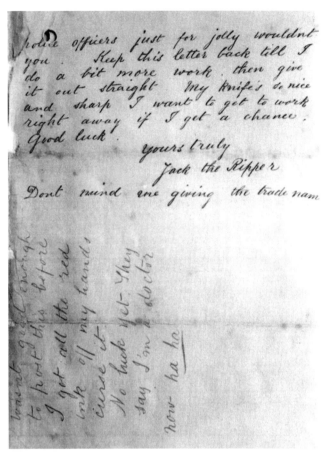

Real or not, the 'Dear Boss' letter is the first time the world hears the name 'Jack the Ripper'.

Such behaviour is not beyond the media of any era and one has to appreciate that these informed detectives would have had inside intelligence that may be long lost to us today. Dr Robert Anderson, head of CID in 1888 went on to say (in his memoirs of 1910) that he knew the name of the journalist who created it but shied from actually naming him publicly for fear of legal action. Others have suggested a plot by the staff of the Central News itself. Whatever the case, the concept of a cynical attempt to keep the momentum of the story buzzing to ensure high newspaper sales is not unreasonable.

Interestingly the letter still has another mystery hanging over it. Shortly after the Ripper files were closed the letter mysteriously disappeared. Vanished without a trace. It was rumoured one of the detectives who worked the case may have taken it as a souvenir. This remained the case for almost 100 years until a mysterious brown envelope turned up addressed to Scotland Yard and given to Bill Waddell, curator of Scotland Yard's crime museum. In the envelope there were papers relating to other infamous crimes plus the missing Dear Boss letter. The source was anonymous and remains so to this day. Where was it all this time? I'd love to know.

The famous letter is now part of the collection of the National Archives in London (the former Public Record Office) where it shares archival space with over two hundred other surviving letters allegedly from the murderer, sent from many places and written in many different styles. As much as these all have their curious appeal, it is the 'Dear Boss' letter which stands as an iconic artefact as it contains the first appearance of 'Jack the Ripper', which almost immediately eclipsed 'Leather Apron' as a name to conjure fear. The name, however, has now become a byword for terror and menace and is often (perhaps awkwardly) used to describe not only the murderer but everything associated with those terrible events of 1888 and beyond.

Chapter 6

The Double Event – Elizabeth Stride

"I saw the body of a woman lying huddled up just inside the gates ... Her
throat cut ear to ear"

Mrs Mortimer, 36 Berner Street

Following the death of Annie Chapman rumours spread like wildfire through
the streets of Whitechapel, and the women who walked the streets after
dark searched the shadows for any sign of the unknown killer. Although this
sense of terror still hung over the East End, the Ripper had been silent for three
weeks by the late evening of 29 September. However, the events that would unfold
later that night would take the already infamous murders to a new level of terror
and be forever known in the annals of crime as "the Double event". The Ripper
would claim two victims in less than an hour.

The Double Event would see both the murders of Liz Stride(left) and Catherine Eddowes (Right)
occurring on the same night, less than 45 minutes apart.

The Former Bricklayers Arms pub at 34 Settles Street. Liz Stride was seen here with a man shortly before her murder.

The first victim was 44-year-old Elizabeth Stride, known locally as "Long Liz" – her body was found at 1.00 am in Dutfield's Yard off Berner Street.

She was born Elisabeth Gustafsdotter in Sweden in 1844, and was first arrested for prostitution in Sweden at the age of 21. Four years later, in 1869, she married John Thomas Stride. Their marriage fell apart in 1877, and by 1885 she was living with a man named Michael Kidney, a waterside labourer. However, their relationship seemed to be over. On 25 September, 1888, she returned to the home they shared, collected her belongings, and left. On 26 September, she was staying in a doss house in Flower and Dean Street in Whitechapel. There, she met the famous Dr Barnardo, who was visiting doss houses in the area. Interestingly, Dr Barnardo would later be one of those to identify her body.

At 11.00 pm on 29 September, Elizabeth Stride was seen in the doorway of a pub called The Bricklayer's Arms on the corner of Settles Street. The building still stands although no longer a pub, it's a convenience store with apartments above. No photograph exists showing what the pub looked like in 1888.

A possible sighting of the Ripper may have occurred around 12.45am by local man, Israel Schwartz.

Her companion was a well-dressed man, described as about 5 feet 5 inches with a black moustache and sandy eyelashes. He wore a billycock hat and appeared to be in good spirits, kissing and hugging Stride and joking with those who passed by – "Watch out, that's leather apron getting round you!" Long Liz and her jovial companion were seen setting off in the direction of Commercial Road a short time later.

By 11.45 pm, Long Liz had moved to Berner Street, where a labourer by the name of William Marshall saw her standing in the door of number 64 on the west side of the street, between Fairclough and Boyd Streets. This time, her companion was a man in a short black cutaway coat and a sailor hat. He was teasing and joking with her. Marshall stated that they kissed, and that the man said, "You would say anything but your prayers."

Yet another man joined Long Liz that evening. By 12.35 am, she was seen with a young man, approximately 28 years old, wearing a dark coat and a deerstalker hat. They were seen outside the International Working Men's Educational Club on Berner Street by Constable William Smith. The man was carrying a parcel, approximately 18 inches long and 6 inches high and wrapped in newspaper.

Berner Street as seen from the junction of Fairclough St. The mounted waggon wheel on the wall, marks the entrance to Dutfield's yard.

Only 10 minutes later, a Jewish man named Israel Schwartz was walking down Berner Street when he noticed a couple arguing in front of the wooden gates of Dutfield's Yard.

Thinking that he was witnessing a domestic spat and wanting to avoid confrontation, Schwartz crossed the road to avoid the couple. He noticed that the man was about 30 years old, with a brown moustache. He stood about 5 feet 5 inches tall. As he passed the gate, the man yelled out "Lipski" – apparently calling to another man standing up the road. The man paused in the act of lighting his pipe and began to follow Schwartz up the street. Fearing for his life, Schwartz began to run and didn't look back until he was sure that he was no longer being pursued. This evidence would later lead police to look for an accomplice to the Ripper's crimes, but their investigations into this second man led nowhere. There has been much debate surrounding the accuracy of Schwartz's statement.

This important eyewitness was not called to testify at the inquest of Elizabeth Stride. Using a Hungarian interpreter, he was interviewed by the Star newspaper, which published his account of events the next day. Some details differ from the police version, but it may be inferred that Schwartz elaborated on his story so that he did not appear a coward by running away. He had witnessed the assault of a woman who – if it was Elizabeth Stride – would be dead within minutes. It's been recently suggested that the word Schwartz heard may have been "Lizzie" instead of "Lipski". If this theory is correct then it shows the attacker knew his victim.

So was he telling the truth? It's difficult to say, he made no attempts to come forward to the police. Several of the newspapers dismissed his statement altogether and his story changes a couple of times, which is usually the sign of someone making up tales.

However if he was telling the truth then the chances of two different men attacking Elizabeth Stride in such a short period of time seems highly unlikely. Thus it's possible that Israel Schwartz is the only eye witness to see Jack the Ripper in the act of murder. The debate will no doubt continue.

At 1.00 am on 30 September, 1888, Louis Diemshutz was returning home with his horse and cart. Diemshutz was a steward at the International Working Men's Club in Berner Street, and had been away most of the day at a market near Crystal Palace. He was sure of the time as he had noted it when he passed the bakers shop on the corner of Berner Street.

The gates to Dutfield's yard were open and as he drove the horse and cart inside his horse shied away from a bundle that was lying roughly 5 feet inside the gateway to the right.

Berner Street as it appears today. A school and playground now occupy the site of Dutfield's yard.

Diemshutz looked down and saw an unusual object on the ground. The yard was about 12 feet wide and dark and he wasn't sure what it was. He would later state that had the horse not shied away he probably wouldn't have noticed it. He prodded the bundle with his whip, but he could not identify it in the dark, so he climbed down from the cart and tried to light a match, and in a moment the wind blew the match out but not before the brief flicker had shown up the body of a woman lying on her side. Unsure whether the body was that of his wife or of a drunk who had stumbled in off the street, he entered the club to investigate further. Upon finding his wife inside, he gathered a few men from the club and went back outside with a candle. Before he had even reached the body, Diemshutz had already noticed blood on the ground close to where the body lay and moments later he and other onlookers found themselves standing over the still warm body of Elizabeth Stride.

She was lying inside the gateway, (according to Dr Blackwell, her feet were three yards from the gateway) her face was turned to the left hand side and facing no more than five or six inches away from the club wall. Her legs drawn up, her feet

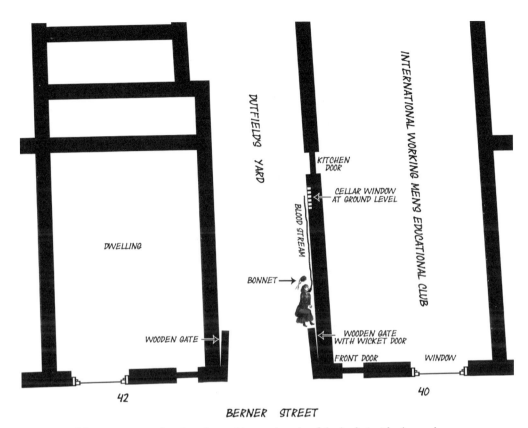

Diagram of the crime scene showing the position and angle of the body inside the yard.

close against the wall. Her dress was unfastened at the neck. Both the neck and the chest were quite warm, as were both the legs and the face. Her hands were cold. The right hand was lying across the chest and was clearly smeared with blood while the left was lying on the ground partially closed and contained a small wrapped paper packet containing cachous.

Although her corpse was still warm, she was clearly dead – her throat had been slit open from the left side of the neck about two and half inches below the jaw, completely severing the windpipe and finishing one inch below the angle of the right jaw. There appeared to be no sign of a struggle.

PC Henry Lamb was on duty in Commercial Road between Christian Street and Batty Street, when he was summoned to the scene. When he arrived there were around 30 onlookers surrounding the body.

Lamb decided to close the yard gates, this was in an effort to stop more onlookers arriving at the crime scene plus it kept all the potential suspects from leaving.

Though blood flowed freely from the wound to Stride's neck, her clothes were not stained with blood, suggesting that she was already lying on her back when the knife bit into her throat. A thorough examination of the body, performed later, would confirm this initial hypothesis – bruising was found on her shoulders which suggested that Stride had been grabbed and thrown to the ground by the killer before he slit her throat. However, there were no additional mutilations to the abdomen or any other part of the body. This fact, combined with the fact that the body was still warm when it was found, suggested that death had occurred only moments before the body was discovered, and that the killer was interrupted in the act of completing his gruesome ritual.

In all likelihood, therefore, Diemshutz entered the yard while the killer was crouched over the body of Elizabeth Stride. His horse shied away, not just from Stride's body, but

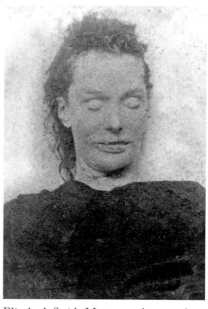

Elizabeth Stride Mortuary photograph.

The old mortuary building where Elizabeth Stride was taken. Today it lies abandoned in the grounds of St George in the East church.

Elizabeth Stride's grave in East London Cemetery.

Diagram outlining the location of Dutfield's Yard today on Henrique Street.

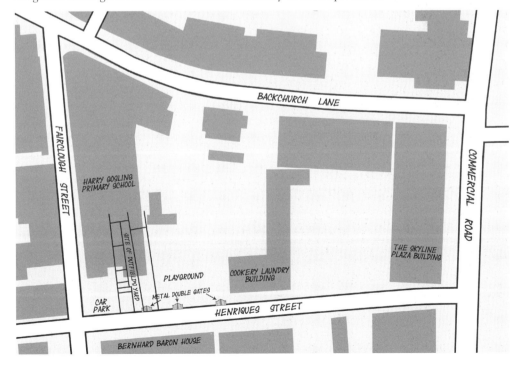

from the living presence of the killer. The Ripper, still clutching his bloody knife, hid in the shadows while Diemshutz initially investigated the body, and escaped while Diemshutz searched the club for his wife. Diemshutz' testimony regarding the strange behaviour of his horse and his own feeling that someone was hiding in the darkness confirm this assumption. This begs the question – what would have happened if the night had not been windy, and the match in Diemshutz's hand had illuminated more of the yard? Diemshutz might have laid eyes on Jack the Ripper himself.

As it was, however, the Ripper escaped the yard, but was forced to leave his most recent victim behind, his ritual incomplete. Fuelled by a rush of adrenaline following his near capture, the Ripper fled the scene, leaving behind the familiar streets of the East End and the swarm of police which would soon descend on Dutfield's Yard. Desperate to slake his bloodlust, he crossed into the City of London and within 45 minutes he set his vicious knife in motion on another victim.

The crime scene of Elizabeth Stride was the first location to be altered, as early as 1909, when Dutfield's Yard, the International Workingmen's Club and all the neighbouring cottages were demolished to make way for the Harry Gosling

These school gates offer something to the imagination as they sit almost on the same spot where the entrance to Dutfields Yard would have been.

The spot where Elizabeth Stride's body was discovered, as it appears today.

Primary School and its playground. In fact, very little of the original Berner Street remains, and it was renamed Henriques Street in the 1960's to commemorate Basil Henriques, a Jewish philanthropist who set up the Bernhard Baron St George Jewish Settlement in the street in the early 20th century.

Several photos were taken of the surrounding streets by Berner Street, these showed the areas set for demolition including Berner Street, so unfortunately the crime scene is taken from a distance. We do however have newspaper descriptions and depictions showing how the yard would have looked.

What's interesting in the modern build is there are two large black gates, roughly in the same location and width of the entrance to Dutfield's Yard. It does give the modern visitor a bit more to work with their imagination.

Chapter 7

The Double Event – Catherine Eddowes

"She was cut up like a pig in the market"

PC Edward Watkins

Mitre Square is less than a 15 minute walk from Henriques Street (formerly Berner Street) where Stride's body was discovered. One of the popular myths of the case is that the Ripper couldn't have reached the second murder site in time unless he had a coach of some kind, but in reality had the Ripper walked directly to Mitre Square at a normal pace after the Elizabeth Stride murder he would have had a good 30 minutes of loitering time before killing his next victim.

Mitre Square lies in the city of London, just off Aldgate High Street. It is the only murder site that took place outside the Metropolitan Police Force jurisdiction. The City of London has its own separate police force, a practice continued to this day.

The Square lies between Mitre Street to the southwest, Duke Street to northeast and St James Place to the northwest.

There were only three ways in and out of Mitre Square. A main entrance from Mitre Street, 25 feet wide and mainly used for delivery of goods from carts and waggons, then there were two narrow paved passages, one called Church Passage, which led from Duke Street and was about 85 feet in length and 5ft wide, the other was called St James Passage, about 55 feet in length and ran from Mitre Square to St James Square.

The square was cobbled and only had three lamps to provide light, one at the main entrance, a freestanding lamp inside the square and another attached to the wall of Church passage. The Square consisted of a mixture of large

Catherine Eddowes.

St Botolph's Church, Aldgate, close to where Catherine Eddowes was found to be drunk and disorderly just 5 hours before her murder.

warehouses including that of Kearly and Tonge, which ran from church passage to St James Passage. In this particular building there was an ex Met policeman called George Morris working as a night watchman. Opposite this to the right was the home of police constable Richard Pearce.

Less than an hour after Elizabeth Stride fell to the Ripper's knife, PC Edward Watkins, member of the City of London police, was on patrol. As he entered Mitre Square around 1.45 am, he shone his lantern into the dark corners as he had done every fifteen minutes all night. This time, however, he made a horrifying discovery – the mutilated body of a woman named Catherine Eddowes.

Forty six years old and originally from Wolverhampton, Eddowes was, like the Ripper's other victims, working as a casual prostitute at the time of her death. For the previous seven years, she had been living with a man named John Kelly, but would often take to the streets to earn extra money when times were hard.

Catherine's journey to Mitre Square and the Ripper's knife began around 8.25 pm on Saturday 29 September. PC L Robinson of the City Police was walking his beat in Aldgate High Street when he noticed that a crowd had gathered on the footpath. He waded through the crowd and found Catherine Eddowes lying on the pavement, drunk out of her mind. When he tried to get her back on her feet she fell, so he called another officer to assist, and the two men took the inebriated woman to Bishopsgate police station and locked her in a cell to sober up.

Just five minutes before Elizabeth Stride's body was discovered, Catherine Eddowes was determined to be sober enough for release. She gave the duty

PC Edward Watkins discovering the horrifically mutilated body in Mitre Square.

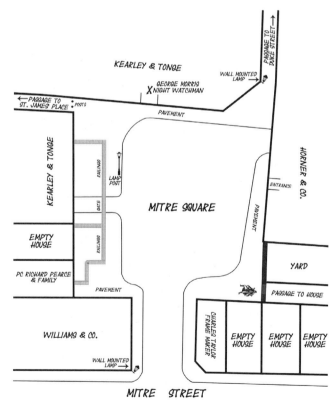

Crime scene diagram outlining Mitre Square and the location of the murder site.

Original crime scene drawing outlining the injuries and mutilations inflicted on the body.

officer her "name" – Mary Ann Kelly – and he let her go. As she walked out the front door around 12.55 am, she called "Good night, old cock!" and turned left toward Houndsditch. She continued on to Aldgate and then walked in the direction of Mitre Square.

Around 1.25 am, PC Watkins walked through Mitre Square, shining his lantern into the corners as usual. Because the square was especially dark, it was the practice of police constables to shine their lanterns into each corner whenever they passed. Seeing nothing out of the ordinary, he proceeded to the night watchman's house, where he paused briefly to heat his tea before continuing his patrol. By 1:45, he had walked the full beat and was returning again to Mitre Square. Shining his lantern into the darkest part of the Square, he made a grisly discovery – the torn and bleeding corpse of Catherine Eddowes.

Horrified, he stared down at the body, which he would later testify was "ripped up like a pig in the market". Eddowes was lying on her back, with her head turned to the left and her arms stretched away from her torso. Her throat had been slashed twice, both cuts reaching back to nick the cartilage of her spine and severing the muscles of her neck. Her dress had been lifted up, exposing the cuts made to the abdomen. This time, it was clear that the killer had been determined to finish his bloody work. Catherine Eddowes had been ripped open from rectum to breastbone. Her stomach was laid

PC Watkins alerting night watchman, George Morris, to the gruesome discovery of yet another ripper victim.

open and her intestines had been lifted out and placed in a pile next to her right shoulder, with a single piece also laid between her body and arm. Later, it would be discovered that her uterus and left kidney had been cut out and taken from the scene by the killer.

Eddowes' face had been mutilated with remarkable precision – her eyelids had been cut and her ear had been severed (it would fall off later in the mortuary). Under each of her eyes, the killer had made a V-shaped incision. Two deep gashes were also made across her face, one of them slicing off the tip of her nose. Looking at the autopsy photographs and sketches made at the time, it is my opinion that the killer was attempting to remove her face in the dark. This escalation in violence would be evident in the later murder of Mary Jane Kelly.

Stumbling away from the corpse, Watkins made for the night watchman's house across the square. The watchman, George Morris, was employed by Kearley and Tong. When Watkins rushed in, he was busy brushing the stairs. Shaken by what he had seen and convinced that the fiend of Whitechapel had strayed in to the City of London, the constable cried, "For God's sake, mate, come to assist me!" Morris grabbed a lantern and followed Watkins back to Eddowes' body. He then ran to Aldgate, blowing his whistle to alert police that the Ripper had struck again.

Mitre Square as it appears today.

Where the body of Catherine Eddowes was found, as it appears today.

Police and reporters, many of whom had been circling around Dutfield's Yard earlier that evening, quickly descended on Mitre Square. Shockwaves of panic were already starting to spread – the vicious killer who had been quiet for a week had now struck twice in the space of a single hour. His second victim had been meticulously and gruesomely slaughtered in less than 15 minutes and he had disappeared into the night without a trace.

The City Police, desperate to find a clue to the identity of the brutal villain who had strayed into their jurisdiction, conducted door to door inquiries, stopped passers-by and questioned numerous men found to be in the area.

Slowly, the police began to piece together small clues. Three Jewish men testified that they had seen a man and a woman around 1.35 am. They were standing at the entrance to Church Passage (which led into Mitre Square), and one of the men, Joseph Lawende, stated that the woman was Catherine Eddowes. Her companion was described as a man of fair complexion; about 5 feet 7 inches tall with a fair moustache and medium build. He was about 30 years of age and wore the peaked

Mitre Square, looking past across the murder site, towards Mitre Street.

cap of a sailor. If this timing was correct, then the killer entered the square with Eddowes just after PC Watkins left, and had less than 15 minutes to complete his ritualistic mutilations before the constable returned. Considering that Watkins saw no one on his first foray into Mitre Square, this scenario does seem plausible. Ironically, another constable was on a nearby beat that took him down Church Passage but not into Mitre Square. PC James Harvey walked down the passage at 1.40 am, and had he shone his lantern into the darkness of Mitre Square, he might have seen the face of Jack the Ripper.

As journalists began to flood the scene, the police brought in sketch artists to record details of the body and Eddowes' body was quickly removed to the mortuary. The corpse was examined by Doctors who concluded that she, like Elizabeth Stride, was killed as she lay on the ground. Death was due to exsanguination caused by the deep cuts to the throat. She would have died within seconds, without making a single sound and the mutilations to her body were done after her death. There was no sign of recent sexual activity anywhere on Catherine Eddowes' corpse.

The "double event" as it became known, caused a frenzy of speculative panic in the press. The self-titled Ripper was back, and had shown prowess, not only at "Ripping", but also at evading the police. He was skilled, meticulous and clever. However, there is no such thing as a perfect crime, and the double event is also famous as the source of a puzzling clue that continues to baffle Ripperologists and has led to one of the most intriguing conspiracy theories of the Whitechapel murder investigations. We will look at this in the next chapter.

Little is known of the investigations undertaken by the City Police into the murder of Eddowes, the only Ripper victim murdered within their jurisdiction; their files were destroyed during World War 2. A brief account was given by Major Henry Smith, the Commissioner of the City Police, in his memoirs, but these are utterly unreliable. The destruction of the case papers is a great loss, for not only might they have given better insight into the approach taken by the city to the Ripper crimes, but they might also have thrown light on a few mysterious and tantalising items of information such as eye witness statements and the names of men they seriously suspected.

Of all the Jack the Ripper murder sites, Mitre Square has been redeveloped most frequently. Once a small enclosure surrounded by imposing grim warehouses, these

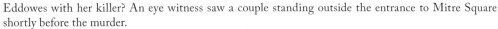

Eddowes with her killer? An eye witness saw a couple standing outside the entrance to Mitre Square shortly before the murder.

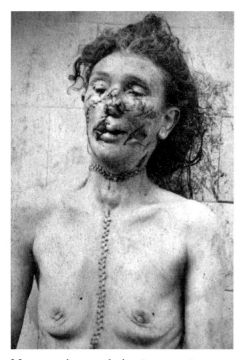

Mortuary photograph showing extensive injuries to face.

Mortuary photograph showing mutilation of throat and abdomen.

buildings were demolished in stages throughout the 1970's to be replaced by modern office blocks. In 1973 the TV show "Barlow and Watt investigate" would show rare footage of the square before the warehouses were demolished and anyone wanting a bit of Ripper memorabilia can grab a copy of Radio Times 7-13 July 1973, where it has the two characters standing at the murder site. More construction footage can be seen briefly in a sequence in the documentary 'Jack the Ripper: The Final Solution', filmed in 1980. Even after the surrounding buildings came down the square still had a little character owing to the survival of old original cobblestones. 'Ripper's Corner', where the body of Catherine Eddowes was found, was for

Mitre Square in the mid 1900's.

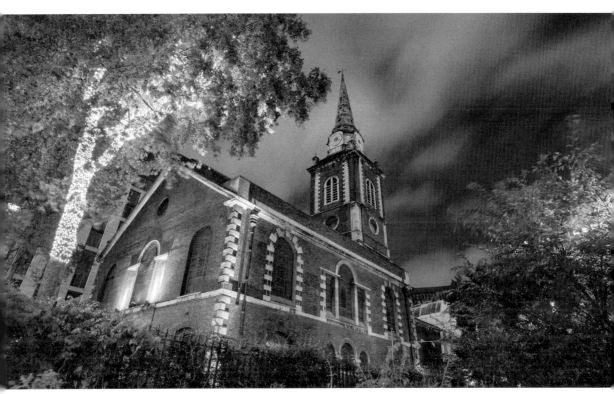

St Botolph's Church Aldgate.

Grave of Catherine Eddowes.

many years accompanied by a small flowerbed and seats, which appeared in 1986. In 2015, the 1970's blocks were demolished after remaining unused for many years and the new, ultra-modern One Mitre Square was completed in 2018, changing the appearance of the square dramatically. The original cobblestones were finally lifted up and disposed of but not before myself and fellow author Mick Priestley had managed to acquire several of them in a quick salvage operation in the dead of night.

Today, Mitre Square now has a much more open appearance, with landscaping features such as grass, trees and seating areas for the City workers to enjoy lunch.

Elizabeth Stride was buried on Saturday, 6 October, 1888 at East London Cemetery Co. Ltd., Plaistow, London, E13. Her grave is number 15509, square 37. The sparse funeral service was provided at the expense of the parish by Mr Hawkes, undertaker.

Catherine Eddowes was buried on Monday, 8 October, 1888 in an unmarked grave in an elm coffin in the City of London Cemetery, (Little Ilford) at Manor Park Cemetery, Sebert Road, Forest Gate, London, E12. She rests in (public) grave 49336, square 318. A round plaque marks the area where she lays and only a few yards from this is the marker dedicated to Mary Ann Nichols who remains buried close by.

Chapter 8

Discovery at Goulston Street

"I do not hesitate to say that if the writing had been left there would have been an onslaught upon the jews, property would have been wrecked, and lives would probably have been lost "

Sir Charles Warren

The night of the Double Event has a third stage, equally important and equally as puzzling. It involves one of the most important clues in the entire case, and could possibly tell us a lot about the killer.

The Metropolitan Police were under significant pressure from all sides even before the double murder on 30 September 1888. Now with the certain publication of the infamous "Dear Boss" letter and the growing criticism from the public press,

Middlesex St (Formerly Petticoat lane) at the junction of Wentworth Street.

Wentworth Model Dwellings on Goulston Street.

it was becoming imperative that they be able to give some sign of progress in the baffling case of the Whitechapel killer. What happened next has been argued about for over 130 years and probably created all those cries of cover up which has engulfed the Ripper case.

In all probability the killer had fled from Mitre Square with only his hands and lower arms covered in blood. The autopsy on some of his victims showed a swollen tongue, the hallmarks of strangulation, which would suggest the killer would wait until alone with his chosen victim and as she went to raise her dress for sex he would lunge forward, grabbing the throat and forcing her to the ground. By the time the first cut to the throat had commenced the victim's heart would have been all but stopped, causing very little outward spray to cover her attacker.

Whilst this would have reduced the likelihood that the killer would have been fully covered in gore, his hands and arms would surely have borne the hallmarks of his grisly deeds.

However, there had as yet been no witness statements that told of a blood-spattered individual hurrying away from the scene of the crime. Nor had anyone reported seeing a man with a large knife or anything else out of the ordinary. Then again, Whitechapel was full of slaughterhouses and butchers plying their trades – men covered in blood with large knives were hardly out of the common way on those dark streets. Moreover, the people of Whitechapel would not have gone out of their way to notice anything – the East End of London was a place where people kept their heads down and their mouths shut in order to survive.

The police were now desperate to find some clue as to the Ripper's identity, particularly after the horrific murders of Elizabeth Stride and Catherine Eddowes. With the press panting at their heels for the latest chilling story, the police spread out, questioning residents and stopping any passers-by in the hopes of finding a lead. These queries came to nothing, and it looked as though the police were stymied once more. But then they got a breakthrough.

At 2.55 am on 30 September, PC Alfred Long of the Metropolitan Police was walking his beat along Goulston Street. Just over an hour before, the ravaged body of Catherine Eddowes had been discovered less than half a mile away. It's a short walk and can be done in five minutes if you walk at a brisk pace. There were

Bell lane as seen from Goulston Street and the junction of Wentworth Street.

also several different routes the killer could have taken which would take about the same time.

PC Long's beat took him past Wentworth model dwellings, it was one of the newer buildings in the area. It was originally constructed to tackle overcrowding and the building housed predominantly refugees from Eastern Europe. As he passed the entrance to 108-119 he shone his lantern into the staircase and noticed something unusual. In the right hand corner, he found a piece of cloth covered in blood and faeces. It later transpired that this piece of cloth was a portion of Catherine Eddowes' apron which had been cut away by the killer and probably used to clean his hands or knife, possibly both.

Another possibility, not mentioned before, is that the killer may have cut himself during the attack on Eddowes and used it to wrap around the wound. I say this because this appears to be the only time a piece of clothing had been cut away from a victim's body. The cloth was heavily saturated in one corner which would imply this was the section that was applied to the wound and then the rest was wrapped around the cloth and hence you get a less saturated but still smeared section. He had attempted to cut her face off in the dark and would no doubt have held her chin whilst cutting downwards. It's highly likely he may have injured himself. It should be noted the killings stopped for over a month following this murder. This could have been a period in which to heal or his wound might lead to suspicions from those around him, he may even have been questioned by police and he decided to lay low.

The entrance to 108–119 Wentworth model dwellings.

The writing on the wall.

Discovering the torn piece of apron and a mysterious message written on the wall in Goulston Street.

This is of course all guess work, but for the first time the police had found a clue to the killer's identity. This cloth had been dropped in the middle of the East End. This implied that, instead of fleeing to the rarefied halls of a West End mansion or racing to the docks to flee aboard a merchant ship, the killer was, in fact, taking refuge in the dark passageways of the same neighbourhood in which he committed his atrocious acts. By all probability his route shows he was heading back into the centre of the killing zone. It occurred to me when writing up this section that most researchers view this case in a modern context, so the Ripper has to discard the cloth before fleeing off into the night, but the whole concept of DNA, finger prints or blood typing would be alien to anyone at that time. There was absolutely nothing that could link that piece of cloth to you if it is no longer in your possession. The Ripper could easily have lived in Wentworth model dwellings and dropped it before going upstairs to his house. I would like to think every room was checked and each inhabitant questioned but no records survive to say if this happened or not.

But the story doesn't end there. There is another piece of this puzzle which is far more befuddling. As the constable raised his lantern further up the wall, he discovered a message scrawled in chalk.

It read, "The Juwes are the men that will not be blamed for nothing".

The location where the clues were discovered is now the 'Happy Days' fish and chip restaurant, the lodgings above are now apartments.

When PC Long reported the discovery of the apron scrap and the cryptic message, several City and Metropolitan police went to see the scene for themselves. It quickly became clear that the message, regardless of who had left it, posed a serious problem. Goulston Street was directly adjacent to the Petticoat Lane Market. Most of the traders there were Jewish, and there had already been problems in the area with anti-Semitic rioting and intimidation due to the Ripper case. Many believed that the Ripper might be Jewish, and violence against Jews around London had become a major public safety issue.

A fierce debate broke out among the officers present. The Metropolitan Police, fearful of further violence against the Jewish population of the area, advocated removing the message immediately. They knew that the area would be swarming with people in only a few hours as early

Author Richard Cobb outside the former entrance where the writing and apron were found.

morning traders started their work day. The City Police, new to the Ripper hunt and keen to avail of any new evidence, argued that this was a crucial clue, and that it was necessary to wait for the light of dawn so that the message could be photographed before it was washed away.

Around 5.30 am, Sir Charles Warren, Commissioner of the Metropolitan Police, arrived on the scene. This was his first visit to the East End since the investigation into the Ripper's killing spree had begun. He entered the doorway and examined the scrawled message himself. To the consternation of the City Police on the scene, he then ordered that the writing be erased immediately. Some sources even claim he wiped the message off the wall himself.

With this one simple act, Sir Charles Warren may indeed have prevented another spate of anti-Jewish rioting, but he also sparked one of the most enduring conspiracy theories related to the Ripper saga.

Why did he remove the message, counter to all protocols and, indeed, all common sense?

We may never know the real answer, but the debate over Charles Warren's actions on that day continues to rage among Ripperologists 126 years later.

A re-creation of the infamous writing sits on the wall of the happy days restaurant.

Today, Wentworth Model Dwellings is perhaps the most famous surviving building which is directly linked to Jack the Ripper. In the years following the murders it gradually fell into disrepair and was lucky not to have been flattened by wartime bombing.

Ironically, the building designed to tackle crowding and poverty became an example of the over populating and overcrowding in post war Britain as the 1970's economic migrants from the Indian subcontinent inhabited the building. There were still communal toilets and wash rooms but bad drainage and sanitary issues promoted disease and soon the building was on the brink of being condemned. By the late 1970's, due to assaults and drug related issues happening on a daily routine, the post office refused to deliver to the address and it seemed this building, just like others, was almost certain to fall victim to the demolition.

By 1982, all the residents had been moved out and the entrances all bricked up. The end seemed near but miraculously the building was saved and given a complete refurbish in the 1990's as apartments again and was renamed Merchant House. Commercial businesses occupied the ground floor and private residence upstairs.

The entrance to 108-119 Wentworth Dwellings, where the clue was found, was converted into an entrance to the new Happy Days fish and chip restaurant and, despite the changes, still features its distinctive original architectural decor over the top, as do all the surviving doorways.

Happy Days Restaurant is a popular haunt for hungry Ripperologists and inside are many photos of the doorway over the years, East End street scenes, Ripper suspects, and a small replica of the infamous graffiti that was found there in 1888. It's certainly worth a visit. Oh and for those fans of the 1980's, you might be interested to learn that Pet Shop Boys 1985 hit West End Girls was filmed outside Wentworth model dwellings.

Chapter 9

From Hell

"Catch me when you can Mr Lusk"
From Hell Letter – 16 October 1888

Following the controversial and shocking events of 30 September 1888, the Central News received a follow-up to the notorious 'Dear Boss' letter. This time it was a postcard, postmarked 1 October and received that same day. It was smeared on both sides with what appeared to be blood and was written in red pencil. Its content indicated knowledge of its predecessor:

"I was not codding dear old Boss when I gave you the tip, you'll hear about Saucy Jacky's work tomorrow double event this time number one squealed a bit couldn't finish straight off. had not the time to get ears for police. thanks for keeping last letter back till I got to work again."
Jack the Ripper

The handwriting appeared identical to the pencilled afterword on the 'Dear Boss' letter and the fact that the writer mentions things that were in the former communication (getting the ears for the police) before being made public pointed to the same author. A transcription of the postcard and parts of the 'Dear Boss' letter were printed in that evening's newspapers and on 4 October, facsimiles were reproduced in the press, a day after official police posters bearing images of the two communications were released: 'Any person recognising the handwriting is requested to communicate with the nearest police station.'

Some have suggested that because the postcard mentions the 'double event' as news yet to be published in the media, the author and the killer were one and the same, thus also confirming the 'Dear Boss' letter as genuine. However, this is not necessarily the case. Although the same author wrote both missives, knowledge of the 'double event' would have been widespread throughout the day of the murders, 30 September. Also, the UK postal service in the Victorian era was considerably more efficient and frequent than it is today, with many more collections (which also included Sundays). The postcard could easily have been written on the 30 September when everybody was heatedly discussing the previous day's events, and posted on the 1 October in plenty of time to arrive at the Central News Agency the same day bearing the postmark of that date.

One interesting development surrounding this postcard was the fact that smeared blood or ink was present and a thumbprint could be seen, prompting one gentleman to write to The Times newspaper on 4 October about the possibility of using fingerprinting as a means to identify the killer:

The surface of a thumb so printed is as clearly indicated as are the printed letters from any kind of type. Thus there is a possibility of identifying the blood print on the letter with the thumb that made it because the surface markings on no two thumbs are alike, and this a low power used in a microscope could reveal.

George Lusk.

An important proposition, but alas one that would not be followed up – fingerprinting for criminal identification had been offered to the Metropolitan Police by Dr Henry Faulds in 1886, but was turned down at the time. It was not until 1902 that the technique was used to convict a thief and three years later to gain a conviction for murder.

There have been well-documented cases of serial killers sending letters to the press and police, often taunting their inability to catch them. Between 1966 and 1974, the Zodiac Killer sent in 20 written communications to the police authorities, often using codes and cyphers, all designed to confuse and taunt those who were trying to apprehend him. The same can be said with the BTK (Bound, Torture & Kill) Killer, Dennis Rader, who made contact with the police, often gloating about his crimes.

Now, no doubt many of the letters were sent by hoaxers, but experts of the case have always felt there may be something genuine about the initial letters that were first sent in. For instance, the first letter signed Jack the Ripper stated that his next victim would have her ears cut off. The next murder that followed, the ears were attacked and severed. A follow-up letter, written in the same hand, claimed that he had not been able to complete his task. Was this a lucky guess by a would-be forger? Or the words of Jack himself?

Others are more sceptical. Andrea Nini, a forensic linguist from the University of Manchester, came to the conclusion that at least two of the infamous letters were

George Lusk's house on Tollet Street.

written by the same person, adding that the writer was not history's most revered serial killer.

So if they are not the words of Jack the Ripper, then who could have written them? There is a theory that the letters are no more than the creation of enterprising journalists at the time of the murders, to keep the story alive and in doing so, sell more papers.

One name that has been brought up in recent times is Thomas Bulling, a central news agency reporter and his colleague Fred Best. Some experts claim there is a similarity in their handwriting to some of the letters received, though this is not the opinion of everyone. If they did write the letter, then it makes perfect sense why the Jack the Ripper letter was sent to their own agency. It gave their paper a fantastic boost and would make them number one in an ever-increasing tabloid war that the Whitechapel murders created.

Unfortunately, at this stage, it is unlikely we will ever know how involved these two men were in creating the myth that we know today but regardless of who wrote the letters, it gave the unknown killer a name that would forever endure in the annals of criminal history.

The question on everyone's lips was, when will he strike again?

October passed peacefully. There were no murders in October of 1888 and nobody really knows why, I put forward a theory earlier suggesting the Ripper may have injured himself in the attack on Catherine Eddowes. Another theory could be because there was now an unprecedented presence of police patrols on the streets, along with dozens of undercover detectives in plain clothes loitering on every street corner. These officers didn't escape the press attention so no doubt the killer had noticed too.

Star reported on Friday 5th

"…Extreme vigilance is now being exercised by the police in Whitechapel. The whole place swarms with detectives and men in uniform … it is feared that the murderer would again select Saturday morning for the perpetration of another crime, and they knew that unless he was caught red handed they would have no evidence against him."

H Division with its 548 beat constables brought in reinforcements from other Divisions. Some detectives were disguised as ordinary labourers and some (more amusingly) dressed up as women and these extra numbers were increased when you add on private detective agencies, city police, citizens patrols and many more local volunteers. The Whitechapel vigilance committee had assigned 50 men to go out at night seeking the killer.

By 3 October all slaughter houses had been searched, every employer questioned. Lodging houses were being told to stay on guard and report any suspicious behaviour. 80000 handbills were posted all across Whitechapel and every household received one.

With all this going on, it's probably no wonder that October passed peacefully.

Except for one man.

Perhaps one of the most notorious events to happen in October 1888 relates to a letter received by George Lusk on 16 October 1888. Lusk was chairman of the Mile End Vigilance Committee, a group of local businessmen who had joined together to 'assist' in the hunt for the Ripper and also to lobby for the offer of rewards for his capture. He was a painter and decorator living in Tollet Street, Mile End and as a result of his group's occasional approaches to the press, his address was known. For a while after the 'double event,' he had been aware of a man lurking around his home on various nights and had approached the police for protection.

On the evening of 16 October, he received a parcel containing what appeared to be half a kidney, accompanied by a letter, written in a semi-literate and untidy fashion. It read:

From hell
Mr Lusk,
Sor
I send you half the Kidne I took from one woman and prasarved it for you tother piece I fried and ate it was very nise. I may send you the bloody knif that took it out if you only wate a whil longer
                    signed Catch me when you can Mishter Lusk

Lusk immediately felt the whole thing was a hoax and, after putting the parcel in his desk drawer for a day, showed it, and its contents, to members of the committee. It was taken to the surgery of Dr Frederick Wiles on Mile End Road and examined by Dr F. S. Reed in his absence. It was then taken to Dr Thomas Openshaw at the London Hospital who concluded that it was half of a left human kidney and little more. Unfortunately, misleading comments were made by F. S. Reed to the press, who stated that Openshaw had claimed it was the kidney of a woman about 45 years of age "and that it had been taken from the body within the last three weeks." Openshaw would later refute this; "He couldn't say, however, whether it was that of a woman, nor how long ago it had

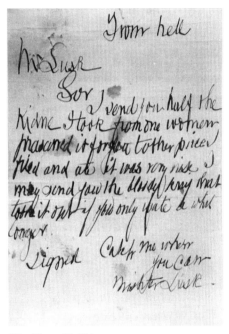

The 'From Hell' letter.

been removed from the body, as it had been preserved in spirits."

The urge to link the organ with the one taken from Catherine Eddowes a few weeks before was inevitable, and led to much contradiction from the experts. City Police surgeon Frederick Gordon Browne believed "that only a small portion of the renal artery adheres to the kidney, while in the case of the Mitre Square victim a large portion of this artery adhered to the body", suggesting he was pointing to the organ as being genuinely from the victim. Others, such as William Sedgwick Saunders, were happy to label it all as "a student's antic. It is quite possible for any student to obtain a kidney for the purpose."

So was the 'Lusk Kidney', as it has become known, genuine?

It seems we will never know, as there has been no definitive evidence from the time to prove it. If any official reports were set down by City Police surgeons such as Gordon Browne, they have yet to be traced, and likely never will be, as most of the City Police documents on the Ripper case were lost to wartime bombing. The portion of kidney was presumed to have been disposed of long ago; there have been stories that it was kept by the London Hospital and disposed of in the 1950s, as well as the possibility that it was kept in the Public Record Office until as late as the 1980s, but neither of these rumours have been substantiated.

If we look at the "From Hell letter" in a modern understanding of serial killers, it's quite possible this could be the work of the actual killer.

Three interesting aspects of the letter stand out. It mentions cannibalism, it's addressed to George Lusk himself and it's not signed Jack the Ripper.

With cannibalism, the writer wants people to believe he has eaten the kidney, to further shock and bring a greater fear to the community. This thought process would go hand in hand with the way the Ripper would leave his victims, exposed and in a demeaning manner, as if to shock all that would gaze upon the body. (100 years later, Peter Sutcliffe aka the Yorkshire Ripper would also create the exact same scenario at his crime scenes). As for addressing the kidney and letter to George Lusk it shows the writer did not seek fame from the global community; if that was what he was after he could have sent it to any national newspaper, he could have signed it Jack the Ripper, just like hundreds of letters that were sent during the murders, but instead he sent it to a local community leader, with the simple words "Catch me when you can".

This points highly to someone who had no real concern with the wider world, had no desire to be called the name he was given and was only focused on the small area of Whitechapel. Just like the Ripper.

So where is the From Hell letter and the kidney today? Sadly, the letter was photographed by the City Police in October 1888 and has officially been missing ever since, although several original copies of the photograph survive, one of which is kept at the London Hospital Museum. The Kidney is a mystery. We presume it stayed up at the London hospital in a jar for some time and then was disposed at a later date. With no knowledge of forensics it's highly doubtful anyone would have kept it unless for a curious collector's item. Perhaps some future researchers can roll their sleeves up and go look for it in the archives of the hospital. You never know your luck.

Chapter 10

Mary Jane Kelly

"The sight we saw, I cannot drive away from my mind.
It looked more like the work of a devil than of a man."
John McCarthy, Landlord of 13 Millers Court

Following the events of the double murder, public hysteria had reached a new high. The women of the East End wrote to the Queen begging for help, and the letters columns of THE TIMES were filled with helpful suggestions from amateur sleuths anxious to help track down the monster who was terrorising Whitechapel. Ideas that ranged from a protective neck cover to protect women from attack, male officers dressed as prostitutes and actual prostitutes being hired

Bloodhounds, Burgho and Barnaby, being put to the test in London.

Scalby Manor in Scarborough. Built 1885 and used as kennels by Edwin Brough, the leading breeder of bloodhounds in the UK during the Whitechapel murders.

as detectives. There's evidence to suggest the police did adopt the latter as a clever way of trapping Jack.

The Washington Post reported –

"A large number of these unfortunates have practically been engaged by the police to aid in hunting down the mysterious fiend. They have been ordered to parade the darkest and least frequented courts and alleys of Whitechapel and Spitalfields, with instructions not to repulse any man who solicits them. They are guaranteed that they will be followed, and that, in the event of any violence being attempted, they shall recieve immediate help. Provided that they can be kept sober, the police consider these women well qualified to act as decoys".

But the most interesting attempt to capture the Ripper was the use of bloodhounds.

It was reported in the Grantham Journal on 13 October 1888 that Sir Charles Warren had watched a private trial with bloodhounds in London's Regent's Park. The dogs had been brought down from Scarborough by dog breeder Mr Edwin Brough after he was contacted by the Met police to see if it was possible for the dogs to:

Seek out a person who has been close to a recent corpse.
Follow the scent on an item of clothing dropped by a criminal
Be able to detect victims blood on the clothing or hands of a criminal

Brough picked two of his finest dogs, Burgho and Barnaby and at 7am with the frost still on the grass they set to work attempting to track down a young man who had been given a 15 minute head start. The dogs worked slowly but proved effective and tracked him down over a mile later. Another trial took place at night with the dogs on a leash and once again proved a success. The following day Sir Charles himself acted as the hunted man in two of the six daily trials and was pleased with the dog's performance. If another murder was to occur in Whitechapel the dogs could be brought in first before anyone was allowed near the body. This was a plan that could possibly work and work well.

Hidden in the overgrown grass area at the rear of Scalby Manor, lies the old kennels which housed Burgho and Barnaby. They are still there at the time of writing.

The grave of Edwin Brough.

Unfortunately the issue of money caused this plan to fail. Understandably Mr Brough wanted the police to buy his dogs but Sir Charles made no assurances that they would be purchased and so the hounds were taken back to Scarborough by their unamused owner.

While researching this book I decided to travel to Scarborough to see if anything remained of Edwin Brough's dog breeding home at Wyndyate (now called Scalby Manor). I'm pleased to report that it is still there to this day. The manor house, built in 1855, is now a stonehouse bar and restaurant but had spent some time as a guest house/ hotel following the years since Edwin Brough and his family lived there. Thanks to fellow ripperologist and researcher Mike Covell, I managed to locate the Brough family grave in the grounds of St Lawrence's church in the village of Scalby before moving on the Scalby manor itself.

Along the way I read reports on the kennels taken at the time by reporters "The Windsor Magazine" reporter A. Croxton-Smith described his kennels in the following terms.

"At the rear of his pleasant Queen Anne house, a couple of miles north of Scarborough, Mr. Brough has a model range of kennels and runs, nothing being left undone that will add to the comfort of the inmates. Every attention is paid to the sanitary arrangements, and the method by which a constant supply of water is carried to each kennel deserves a word of praise."

In 1901 "The Scarborough Magazine" made the following observations.

"From the house we passed through the beautifully kept grounds to the extensive yards in the rear, where Mr. Brough has a model range of kennels and runs, nothing being left undone that will add to the comfort of the inmates. Each kennel has its own run in front, allowing the pair of occupants plenty of room in which to exercise. At present Mr. Brough has about twenty adult hounds and a similar number of pups."

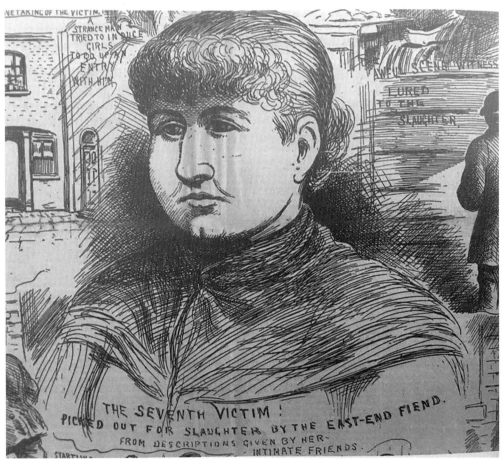

The real Mary Jane Kelly? According to the newspaper, this image was drawn from descriptions given by her close associates.

Dorset Street.

What made this trip even more amazing was discovering the original brick dog kennels that once housed Burgho and Barnaby are still there in the rear yard of the

manor, exactly as described by the press over 120 years ago. Although the area of the kennels now is overgrown and the gates rusted and in bad condition it has a real trapped in time feel to it.

Sadly the threat of demolition now looms over this overgrown patch and I believe plans are in place to have this part of the building listed and kept safe. Let's hope so.

In 1902 Edwin dispersed his kennels and moved with his wife Helen to Hastings in Sussex. He died there in 1829. His obituary was recorded in "The Times"

For me personally I find the story of these two dogs quite fascinating

ENTRANCE TO BLOOD ALLEY.

The entrance to Millers Court.

Number 13 Millers Court.

and I often think what could have been, because the real tragedy of this story is shortly after the dogs were taken from London the Ripper committed his final and most ghastly murder. The murder of Mary Jane Kelly on 9 November 1888, happened in a small locked room and here he spent more time with a victim than he ever had before. If there was ever a chance to put those dogs to the test, it would have been then. Would they have caught the Ripper? We will never know.

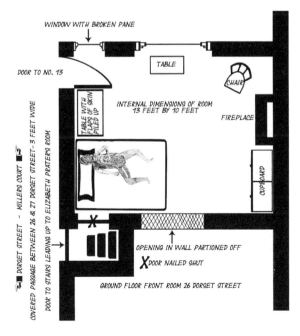

Mary Kelly remains the mystery victim in the Ripper case. Very little is known about her and what we do know is based on tales she told friends in the last years of her life. The common story told is that she was born in Limerick, Ireland in and around 1863. As a child she moved with her family to Wales and, at the age of 16, married a pit worker named Davies, but he was killed a few years after in a pit explosion. Mary then moved

Crime Scene map of the interior of 13 Millers Court and position of the body.

towards Cardiff for almost a year before ending up in a west end brothel in 1884. Stories have her going to France but she returned and now was in the East End and living in a lodging house in Thrawl Street.

It was around this time when she met Joseph Barnett, a market fish porter, and the two of them set up home together. With bills unpaid they would drift from one house to another, until finally around March 1888 they moved into 13 Miller's Court, Dorset Street.

Dorset Street was a narrow road running between Commercial Street and Crispin Street with a notorious reputation. It was known simply as the worst street in London. Rumours had it that the police preferred not to go down

Mary Jane Kelly crime scene photograph – one the earliest examples of C.S.I images taken in the UK.

it unless in teams of four. An area of the worst depravity in the East End. The poorest doss houses, prostitutes and thieves, all had existed along this road.

13 Millers Court was entered through a small narrow brick archway running in between numbers 26 and 27 Dorset Street. It ran about 21 feet into a small cul de sac of smaller houses. Number 13 was actually just a room which had been formed when a partition was put up in the pantry of number 26 Dorset Street. The landlord was a shopkeeper named John McCarthy.

Mary was known to have a fierce temper when drunk, which was often, and in the days leading up to her death Mary and Joseph's relationship had broken down, another fierce argument on 30 October resulted in one of the windows of the room being smashed and Joseph Barnett finally moving out. Although they were now no longer living together Joseph would visit her every day right up until the night of her death. It was also around this time that the key to 13 Millers Court went missing and access to the room could be gained by reaching in through the broken window and pulling back the catch on the door. My own opinion is the key was lost by Mary or Joseph on a typical drunken night out, an argument ensued and the window was smashed to gain entry and it stayed that way.

On the night of 8 November 1888, Barnett would visit Kelly for apparently the last time. According to his statements "I last saw her alive between half-past seven and a quarter to eight on Thursday night last, when I called upon her."

Dorset Street no longer exists. A modern office block now sites over the site.

Maria Harvey had been staying with Kelly a couple of nights during the week and claimed to have been in 13 Millers Court at the time Barnett visited. Before leaving the pair alone in the room she said "Well, Mary Jane, I shall not see you this evening again," She also claimed to have left with her with two men's dirty shirts, a little boy's shirt, a black overcoat, a black crepe bonnet with black satin strings, a pawn-ticket for a grey shawl, upon which 2s (shillings) had been lent, and a little girl's white petticoat.

Later that night Mary Kelly was drinking heavily, along with other women, in the Horn of Plenty pub and would be seen later by her neighbour, Mary Ann Cox. She was entering her room with a man, later described as heavily built, 5ft 5in, blotchy skin, a thick carroty moustache and wearing what appeared to be a billycock hat. Cox would later state she heard Mary singing the ballad, "Only a violet I plucked from mother's grave."

The final sighting of Mary Kelly that night was at 2.00 am, when George Hutchinson, a resident of the Victoria Home for working men was passing Flower and Dean Street. He met Mary and she immediately asked if he had any money he could spare her. Having already spent his money earlier he refused and Mary went on her way up Commercial Street. It is here that Hutchinson claimed to have seen a second man approach Kelly. He put his hand on her shoulder and they both laughed. The couple then proceeded to walk back up Commercial Street towards Hutchinson and Millers Court. Here, Hutchinson was so intrigued by the man's appearance he stooped down as the couple passed, so he could see under the man's hat to get a good look at his face. Later he would give a very detailed description to the police.

According to Hutchinson, Kelly's companion was described as aged about 35, 5ft 6in. pale complexion with dark eyes and eyelashes. A small moustache with both ends slightly curled up, dark hair. Very surly looking. He was wearing a long dark coat with astrakhan collar and cuffs, a light waistcoat, dark trousers, dark felt hat, button boots and gaiters with white buttons. He also had a thick gold chain, a horse shoe tie pin and black tie. According to Hutchinson the man was very respectable in appearance.

The couple proceeded to walk into Dorset Street and disappeared into Millers Court. Hutchinson followed close by and waited outside for 45 minutes waiting for

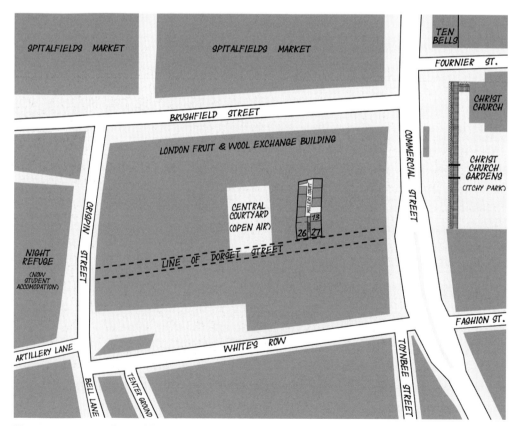

Using survey maps it's possible to pinpoint the location of the crime scene today.

the man to re-emerge. Some theories suggest he may have been waiting to see if Mary would service him for free.

It was now 3.00 am and Hutchinson decided to move on, the Victoria Home for working men had closed for the night so he was going to have to find elsewhere to stay. Had he stayed a bit longer it's possible he may have heard Kelly's final words.

At 4.00 am, Elizabeth Prater, who lived in a room above Kelly, was woken by the cry of "Oh Murder" but as these were quite common shouts in and around the area, she turned over and went back to sleep.

At 10.45 am on 9 November, the day of the Lord Mayor's parade, landlord John McCarthy sent his assistant Thomas Bowyer to collect the rent from Miller's Court. Mary Kelly was thirty shillings in arrears. Thomas Bowyer entered Millers Court and knocked twice on the door of number 13. He got no answer. Not to be outdone and sensing she may be trying to avoid him, he went round to the window and the broken window pane, still there from the previous fight Kelly had had with Barnett only 9 days before. He pulled out the paper that was blocking the hole and he proceeded to put his hand in and pulled back the curtain. He stared into the room and the sight that stared back at him was one of such sheer horror that it would haunt him until his dying day.

In the centre of the office block an open walk through allows visitors to stand on the spot where Dorset Street once stood.

Just beyond these glass walls is the location of Millers Court as it appears today.

There in her small room, on her bed, lay the remains of Mary Kelly. She had been butchered like an animal. Bowyer, in a scared panic, went immediately back to John McCarthy and the landlord himself went to gaze upon the horrific sight. He would later state:

> "The sight we saw I cannot drive from my mind. It looked more like the work of a devil than of a man. I had heard a great deal about the Whitechapel murders, but I declare to God I had never expected to see such a sight as this."

McCarthy then instructed Bowyer to go swiftly to nearby Commercial Road police station and raise the alarm. Within a short time, another area of the East End would be alive with crowds and onlookers. This time the police waited before entering the crime scene, they wanted to get blood hounds in to help track down the murderer but after several hours wait it was soon realised they would not be coming. At 1.30 pm the decision was made to enter the room with John McCarthy himself using a pick axe to prise open the door.

The carnage was even more dreadful at close range. The room was about 12 feet square, containing two tables, a chair and a bed. On the bedside table was a mound of hacked-out flesh. The cause of death was as usual a deep cut to the neck, which had nearly severed the head from the body. The abdomen had been ripped open and both breasts cut from the body. The left arm, like the head, hung to the body by the skin only. The nose had been cut off, the forehead skinned and the thighs stripped of flesh. The liver and entrails had been wrenched away. The liver was found placed between the feet of the victim. The flesh from the thighs and legs, together with the breast and nose, had been placed by the murderer on the table, and one of the dead woman's hands had been placed inside her stomach.

No policeman who saw the body could ever forget it and many memoirs echoed one Inspector, Walter Dew, when he later wrote

"As my thoughts go back to Millers court…No savage could have been more barbaric. No wild animal could have done anything so horrifying."

A thorough search of the room revealed no clues to the Ripper's identity but there were other points of interest. In the fireplace were the smouldering remains of a large fire, containing the remnants of burnt women's clothing, which included a

13 Millers Court, the room where Mary Kelly was murdered, is now located inside the lift shaft of elevator B.

The body of Mary Kelly is buried in St Patricks Roman Catholic Cemetery. The exact location is unknown but a small marker has been placed within the area.

skirt and a hat. Kelly's clothes were folded over a chair. Some suggest the clothing was burnt to provide light for the killer to work with but this doesn't hold up when properly looked at. The clothing would have burnt up fairly quickly and thus fail to provide sustained fuel to light up the room for a great deal of time and if that was the intention of the killer he seems to have ignored Kelly's clothes, which would have given him a few more minutes of light. Maybe Kelly burnt the clothing herself to keep warm before going to bed. It's a mystery that hasn't been properly explained.

According to the St. James Gazette 10 November 1888,

"The bed sheets had been turned down, and this was probably done by the murderer after he had cut his victim's throat".

This suggests the bed sheets were up over her body before the attack. There were also stab marks in the sheet, where her head would be and anyone looking at the crime scene photograph can clearly see what appear to be defence wounds on Kelly's arms. It seems the woman was asleep in bed at the time and attacked as she slept. The clothes folded neatly on the chair would also support this conclusion. We know the killer doesn't have sex with his victims, according to the doctor's reports, so he was not sleeping next to her at the time and it's extremely doubtful Kelly would let a strange man sleep the night in her room during the Jack the Ripper manhunt.

It seems highly likely the killer had let himself in by placing his hand through the broken window, pulling back the catch. He then attacked and murdered her in her sleep.

At 3.50pm on the day of the murder, a one horse carrier cart with a tarpaulin cover was driven into Dorset Street and halted outside Millers Court. From the cart was taken a long shell/coffin box, dirty and scratched with constant use and brought into the room to collect Mary Kelly's body. The news that the body was about to be removed caused a great rush of people from all the courts in Dorset Street and the police struggled to hold onlookers back from the Commercial street entrance. Where anger and violence had greeted the news of previous murders, this was a much more sombre affair. As one reporter said "The crowds that pressed round the

Following the funeral of Mary Kelly, mourners, including Joseph Barnett, held a wake at the Birkbeck Tavern at 46 Langthorne road, just next to St Patricks Cemetery.

Shoreditch Town hall. The inquest into Mary Kelly's murder was held here on 12 November 1888.

van was of the very humblest of class, but the demeanour of the poor people was all that could be desired. Ragged caps were doffed, and slatternly looking women shed tears, as the shell, covered with a ragged looking cloth, was placed in the van."

Mary Jane Kelly was buried in a public grave Monday, 19 November, 1888 at St Patrick's Roman Catholic Cemetery, Langthorne Road, Leytonstone E11. Her grave was no. 66 in row 66, No family could be found to come to the funeral and more than 130 years later researchers are still no closer to discovering who the real Mary Jane Kelly actually was.

As Kelly was laid to rest few, if any, would realise this would be considered the last Jack the Ripper murder and the beginning of a gruesome Victorian legacy which still lingers around the East End today. After 6 months, the investigation gradually wound down. The expensive Special Forces patrols drafted into Whitechapel would be withdrawn by March 1889. Press and public interest in the Ripper waned and by 1892 the case had ground to a halt. Over the next decade or so, the various officers central in the investigation retired from the police force and witnesses vanished into obscurity, along with friends of the victims. As for the Ripper it was assumed by many that the killer had either died, was locked away in asylum somewhere or had fled the country. Several of the officers in charge of the case did put forward theories as to who the Ripper may have been but the fact they all named different individuals simply proves the case was never solved to their complete satisfaction.

The files were kept from the public until the mid-1990s but it was commonly known researchers could access them from the mid 1970s. Sadly there wasn't the strict code of conduct in the police as they have today and it is suspected, over the 100 years they sat gathering dust on the shelf, many of the files relating to the Ripper case were taken out or misplaced by retired officers, researchers and archive thieves. It does make you wonder what might still be out there.

Sixteen years later and Dorset Street was renamed Duval Street in 1904, mainly to eradicate its terrible reputation, as a number of other murders took place there after Mary Kelly's in November 1888. When author Dan Farson was researching the Ripper story for his own book (and TV show, Farson's Guide to the British) he encountered a woman who had lived in number 13 with her mother following the Kelly murder. She would claim that for years the police were constantly bringing visitors to the site to show them where it all happened and that the blood stains remained on the wall of the room regardless of how much they were scrubbed.

Miller's Court was closed off during the first World War as a health hazard and it, and the entire north side of the street, was demolished in 1928 to make way for the Spitalfields Market Fruit and Wool Exchange, which opened the following year. The south side, still with some of its original doss-houses, came down in the 1960s and the whole street became a wide lorry park for vehicles servicing the market. When the White's Row car park was built in the early 70's, Duval Street (though officially unnamed and a private road) was back on the map, staying this way until 2015 when the rear of the exchange and the car park were demolished to make way for an ambitious new development which filled the entire block, thus eradicating that most notorious of streets. On Crispin Street, opposite where Dorset Street once emerged, is Lillian Knowles House, now accommodation for students, but previously the Providence Row Night Shelter, where some would have it that Mary Kelly lived for a brief period of time. However, this appealing rumour has never been confirmed.

For those seeking to see where it all happened, the new office build that occupies the site today has a public thoroughfare running through its centre. Inside are markings on the ground which point out how the original street would have run. As for 13 Millers Court, the room where Mary Kelly's body was found is now replaced by a triple lift shaft in the main office block. Dozens of workers use it every day as they arrive for work, blissfully unaware that they are standing where arguably the East End's most notorious murder took place.

Chapter 11

Were There Other Victims?

The list of victims, that we refer to as being the Canonical Five, has dominated the perceived knowledge of Jack the Ripper studies for decades. This has been the understanding since the 1950's and became ingrained in popular culture around the 1970's with author Stephen Knight's book "The final solution". Knight's theory would introduce the wider world to the idea that Jack the Ripper was a Royal doctor sent out to silence a blackmail plot aimed at the royal family. It's true to say that even today this theory is the number 1 image in the public conscious, despite the fact there has never been any evidence to support it.

So as far as the public are concerned there were five murders and five murders only. However, in the Whitechapel Murder file itself there are in fact eleven murders that took place between 1888 and 1891. So let us examine the cases of the remaining victims.

Rose Mylett

The death of Rose Mylett has intrigued many Ripper researchers today with some questioning why it should even be included on Scotland Yard's Whitechapel Murders list in the first place. Whether it was 'murder by person or persons unknown' has always been debatable. Catherine 'Rose' Mylett was 29 years old when she died in Clark's Yard off Poplar High Street on 20 December 1888, the location being ill-lit and considered a relatively dangerous neighbourhood. The yard itself was around eight to ten feet wide and after 20 yards it opened up much wider to allow for workshops and stables. This yard was eventually destroyed in 1966 to make way for the building of Norwood House.

The last time Mylett was seen alive was between 1.45 and 2.30am walking past The George pub in Commercial Road. The witness, Alice Graves, said that Mylett was visibly drunk (she was often intoxicated, earning her the nickname 'Drunk Lizzie Davis') and accompanied by two men.

At 4.15am, her body was found in the darkness of Clark's Yard by Sergeant Robert Golding, who immediately recognised her as one of the local prostitutes. She was lying on her left side, her left cheek on the ground, her left arm underneath her and her left leg was slightly drawn up. A little blood could be seen trickling from her nostrils. Importantly, there were no signs of mutilation or any other injury, Mylett's clothes were not disarranged and the presence of money in her dress pocket suggested that robbery had not been a motive in any attack on her by a third party. In fact, it appeared on examination of the area surrounding the body that a struggle had not taken place.

A small clue was noticed in the mortuary when a mark around the neck was discovered by a mortuary keeper which appeared to have been made by a cord of some type. Further examination of the body during the post-mortem strongly pointed to death by strangulation in the opinion of Dr Matthew Brownfield. However, the police opinion was that she had died of natural causes, a bizarre conclusion considering Dr Brownfield's evidence. Even more embarrassing was the suggestion that the Ripper may have been responsible. In fact, one newspaper made the unsubstantiated claim that Dr George Bagster Phillips was of the opinion that he saw the same hand at work as that of the murder of Annie Chapman the previous September. In fact, professional opinion regarding Mylett's death saw the authorities in disarray.

The problem, it seems, was a breakdown in communication. The police had not found any sign of violence on Mylett's body or any sign of a struggle in Clark's Yard when they conducted the initial examination of the scene, and thus foul play was not suspected. But when an inspector spoke to Dr Brownfield, the medical man's opinion that murder had taken place was not communicated further and thus the natural causes conclusion was still 'in the system'. When Brownfield's opinion that murder was the cause of death and that the Ripper's involvement was suggested at the public inquest, the police found themselves in an embarrassing situation.

Dr Thomas Bond was instructed by Assistant Commissioner Robert Anderson to make his own examination and his conclusions did little to assist in the controversy: Bond felt that strangulation had been the cause of death but, astonishingly, that Mylett had fallen down while drunk and had compressed her larynx against the neck of her jacket, and that the mark described as the mark of a cord must have been produced by the rim of the collar of her jacket. A presumably confused and frustrated inquest jury nonetheless returned the verdict of 'wilful murder' which again put the opinions of some of the top Scotland Yard men on a very uneven footing. It almost felt that the police, painted into a corner, had done everything they could to push for a verdict of accidental death.

The case of Rose Mylett remains a tricky one. Where it was highly unlikely that Jack the Ripper was responsible for this homicide (if it indeed was a homicide), it did demonstrate that the Ripper would remain a convenient scapegoat for the deaths of prostitutes for some time to come. Indeed, another murder the following year would certainly see one distinguished surgeon put the blame squarely in the hands of Jack the Ripper.

Alice McKenzie

Just before 1.00 am on the wet morning of 17 July 1889, PC Walter Andrews found the dead body of 40-year-old Alice McKenzie in Castle Alley, a dingy narrow passageway which ran from the north side of Whitechapel High Street between Goulston Street and Commercial Street. The body was found on the western side of Castle Alley, next to the Whitechapel Baths house.

The cause of death was later discovered to be a severance of the carotid artery, the result of two cuts in the neck, and there were also a number of superficial stabs and cuts to the lower abdomen. This murder was interesting in that the injuries were inflicted upon the same areas of the body associated with the crimes of 'Jack the Ripper' and, as a result, a number of officials were of the belief that the Whitechapel murderer had struck again. Although Dr George Bagster Phillips believed that a certain degree of anatomical knowledge was possessed by the killer, he did not think that the Ripper had committed this particular crime. Dr Thomas Bond, on the other hand, stated rather categorically:

> "I see in this murder evidence of a similar design to the former Whitechapel murders, viz. sudden onslaught on the prostrate woman, the throat skillfully and resolutely cut with subsequent mutilation, each mutilation indicating

The former wash houses on Castle Alley, where Alice McKenzie was found murdered.

sexual thoughts and a desire to mutilate the abdomen and sexual organs. I am of opinion that the murder was performed by the same person who committed the former series of Whitechapel murder."

This opinion was also one taken by Chief Commissioner James Monro, who felt that the murderer of Alice McKenzie was "identical with the notorious Jack the Ripper of last year."

McKenzie, known as 'Claypipe Alice' owing to her pipe-smoking habit, was certainly from the same category of victims as the previous ones: a resident for many years of a lodging house in Gun Street, Spitalfields, she had managed to hold down a regular relationship with John McCormack, and although she was deemed to be an industrious woman who worked as a charwoman, she was known to work the streets on occasion, leading police to consider her a common prostitute. The scene of the crime, Castle Alley; a narrow secluded thoroughfare with a mean reputation, was perfect for the Ripper to commit the crime. And as with previous killings, great risk of capture was ever present: PC Andrews, who found her body, had passed the same spot less than thirty minutes previously and just prior to that, PC Joseph Allen actually stood there having a snack. Close by on Wentworth Street was a police Sergeant and of course, a number of residents in the properties close by. Interestingly, Sarah Smith, deputy of the adjacent Wash House, who was reading by candlelight in bed by a window that overlooked the alley, claimed to have heard nothing unusual that night until the sounding of PC Andrews' whistle on discovering the body.

The police obviously took this murder seriously, despite the differences of opinion as to who was the perpetrator and, as a result, Chief Commissioner Monro drafted in 42 extra officers into the area. There had also been some press reports stating that just prior to the incident, a letter had been received by police from 'Jack the Ripper', in which the writer said that he was "about to resume his work."

Was Alice McKenzie a true victim of Jack the Ripper? I guess we will never know, but this murder certainly bears enough resemblance to those committed the previous year to be considered as yet another atrocity from the Whitechapel Murderer

Visiting the murder site today you can see Castle Alley has been renamed Old Castle Street and only the façade of the old wash house remains, looking up you can still see the words, 'WASH. HOUSES.' engraved in the stone. The rest of the building was demolished around the mid 1990's to make way for the Trades Union Congress Library which forms part of the London Metropolitan University.

Pinchin Street torso

Perhaps one of the most curious incidents during the period of the Whitechapel murders of 1888-91 was the grisly discovery of a woman's headless torso under a railway arch in Pinchin Street, Whitechapel, in the early morning of 10 September 1889. PC William Pennett discovered the torso at 5.15 am when he was aware of an unpleasant smell emanating from the arch, which lay close to Backchurch Lane.

Pinchin Street lies north of Cable Street and runs from Back Church Lane to Christian Street. Interestingly the murder site is only a few minutes walk from where Elizabeth Stride was murdered, a year before, on Berner Street. Pinchin street consisted mainly of dwellings and vacant grounds and on the south side was a line of railway arches leading to the Commercial Road Goods Depot.

When found, the body, missing head and legs, had already begun to decompose and was found wrapped in an old chemise. Apart from the missing limbs, the abdominal area had been badly mutilated and it was believed the woman had been killed more than 24 hours previously.

The press were keen to speculate that the abdominal mutilations bore shades of Jack the Ripper and it was also said that the uterus of the woman was missing,

The Pinchin Street torso was discovered inside the second archway to the right. Today it's been bricked up and forms part of a residential home and art studio.

making it very tempting to link this awful crime with the Whitechapel murderer, particularly as it was discovered in the Ripper's hunting ground. However, Sir Melville Macnaghten, Chief Constable of the Metropolitan Police at that time, noted that "the head and legs had been severed in a manner identical with that of the woman whose remains were discovered in the Thames, in Battersea Park, and on the Chelsea Embankment on 4 June of the same year."

Macnaghten was referring to a series of other murder mysteries known today as the Thames Torso Murders, where over a several year period, various pieces of women were found in locations close to the River, or indeed floating in it. One discovery was made in the foundation works of the New Scotland Yard building in Whitehall, which was then under construction. Other remains were found at Rainham and Macnaghten was of the belief that the Pinchin Street case bore unquestionable similarities with this series of unsolved crimes. It seems that the police were very cautious about suggesting that the Pinchin Street discovery had anything to do with the Ripper.

But like the Whitechapel murders and the Thames Torsos, the perpetrator of these grisly deeds was never found.

Three men, who were found to be sleeping rough in an adjacent archway, were brought in for questioning but released when they were able to give a satisfactory account of themselves and their reasons for being there. And the mystery of the identity of the dead woman herself remained unanswered: apparently, the hands showed no signs of manual labour and sadly these were the only clues the police could muster, for there were no other distinguishing features from which a positive ID could be made. For a brief time, the woman was believed to be a lady called Lydia Hart, a prostitute who had apparently been missing for some time, however she was soon located, apparently recovering in a hospital after "a bit of a spree." Suggestions that the body was that of another missing girl, Emily Barker, came to nothing.

Although it is very unlikely that the Pinchin Street Torso had anything to do with Jack the Ripper, it remains yet another murder mystery discovered in the East End during that terrible period and thus it sits on the full list of Whitechapel Murders of 1888 to 1891, as they were perceived at that time.

The entrance to the archway in Pinchin Street where the torso was found has long been bricked up and can only be entered from Back Church Lane. Officially known as 10 Back Church Lane, the interior of the archway is now used as an events gallery.

Frances Coles

On 13 February 1891, Frances Coles, a 32-year-old prostitute, was found close to death under a grimy dark railway arch (with the curiously pretty name of Swallow Gardens) between Royal Mint Street and Chamber Street in Whitechapel. Her throat had been cut. PC Ernest Thompson, a newly appointed Constable, made the

Swallow gardens as it appears today. There is no longer a cut through access under the railway tunnel.

discovery on what was the first solo beat of his police career and just before finding Coles, had heard the sound of somebody running away from the scene. Looking at the body before him, Thompson believed he saw her eye move, suggesting she was still alive, and it is now believed that she died on the stretcher on her way to the London Hospital.

The archway where Frances Coles was found is still there to this day. The Chamber Street entrance to the archway can still be seen and is now a commercial premise. The narrow, dark and desolate street, on any given night still portrays a grim atmosphere even now and is a typical setting for what the public imagine Jack the Ripper's London to look like.

Frances Coles, from Bermondsey, is believed to have worked as a prostitute in the East End for some eight years but, like many women, this did not stop her striking up more durable relationships. At the time of her death, Coles was with James Sadler, a ship's fireman whom she had known on and off for some years, a rather gruff, often violent man who frequently indulged in excessive drinking. The night before her death the couple had been on a formidable pub crawl and had become drunk and emotional. In Thrawl Street, Sadler was set upon and robbed, and the fact that Coles never came to his assistance led them to argue, after which they went to their lodgings in White's Row. After a short while, Sadler left.

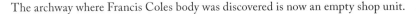

The archway where Francis Coles body was discovered is now an empty shop unit.

From then on, after being refused admittance to his ship, the SS Fez, Sadler found himself in a number of drink-fuelled altercations in the area around Royal Mint Street and the docks, one of which led to minor medical treatment and a short stay in the London Hospital. He was also robbed a second time that night along the Highway in Wapping. Later, he was seen in a doss-house selling a knife to a fellow lodger, and this became one of several reasons to arrest him on suspicion of Coles' murder. There was also briefly the suggestion that he may have been Jack the Ripper, however investigations made unto his whereabouts in 1888 put him at sea on the relevant dates, but he still remained suspect number one for the killing of Frances Coles. He was charged on 16 February.

With excellent representation from the Seaman's Union and the lack of any concrete evidence linking him to the murder, James Sadler was later acquitted of the crime. Also, the knife he had sold was apparently incapable of inflicting Coles' wounds and it was believed that in his then incredibly intoxicated condition, Sadler would have been incapable of efficiently inflicting them.

Two interesting developments followed this incident. Firstly, PC Thompson, when discovering the body, was forbidden by policing rules to leave the body until help had arrived, and thus was unable to follow the footsteps he had heard leaving the scene; his belief that he may have let Jack the Ripper run free would haunt him for the rest of his short life. Secondly, in 1900 he received fatal stab wounds from a man named Abraham Barnett after breaking up an altercation on Commercial Road.

So were the non-canonical victims in fact victims of Jack the Ripper? Potentially some were, but others weren't and researchers cannot agree. So, like most studies of ripperology will conclude, It's up to you to evaluate the evidence and make your own mind up.

Chapter 12

So Who Was He?

"It's often said there's a set of records kept here or a set of records at the Home Office that tell us who it is. That's a nonsense….. I can safely say we do not keep a set of records here at New Scotland Yard who tell us who Jack the Ripper is. We do not know, we never solved it."

William Wadell, curator of Scotland Yard's museum of crime.

So now we come to that final chapter where (if this was a normal Jack the Ripper book) we would reveal the name of history's most elusive serial killer. Sadly, it's here were we must disappoint you. In 1888, there were no forensics or DNA, there was no signed confession and no convictions in the case of Jack the Ripper. Thus no conclusive evidence exists to tell us who it was.

But that doesn't mean we can't explain the character of the killer.

With the passage of time it is possible to identify the type of person the Ripper may have been. Psychopaths and sociopaths are popular psychological terms when describing violent monsters which haunt our worst nightmares. In modern culture, characters such as Hannibal Lecter from the movie "Silence of the Lambs" and even Norman Bates in the Alfred Hitchcock classic "Psycho" have painted an image of what real monsters could look like into our minds. But what makes them who they are?

In the 1970s, the Federal Bureau of Investigations (FBI) started a specialised unit to monitor and record the behavioural characteristics of serial killers. Since then, the art and craft of criminal profiling has become a household name, largely due to books, documentaries and the recent television hit show "Mindhunter". Currently showing on Netflix, the show is based in part on the writings of best-selling author Mark Olshaker and legendary FBI profiler John Douglas.

Douglas was one of several pioneering FBI agents who basically invented computer-based, modern-day criminal profiling in the 1980s. His research has aided law enforcement across the globe in capturing some of the world's most dangerous killers. But could it solve the most infamous cold case in the world?

In 1988, John Douglas and Roy Hazelwood of the FBI were asked to use their acquired knowledge and collected data to prepare a psychological profile of the Ripper, made especially for the television documentary "The Secret Identity of Jack the Ripper".

Poverty still prevails even today in the darker haunts of Whitechapel.

Taking all the known evidence, eyewitness statements and police reports, they looked once again at the Jack the Ripper murders. They concluded the following features of the profile:

- Local, resident male in his late 20s
- Probably employed (murders generally occurred at the weekends)
- Single, without family ties (murders took place between 12.00 am and 6.00 am)
- Of low class (murders showed lack of care/attention to detail)
- Not surgically skilled or possessing anatomical knowledge
- Probably known to the police as a past offender
- Seen by family and acquaintances as a loner
- Probably abused or deserted as a child by his mother

What is interesting about the profile is that it closely resembled another profile carried out at the time of the murders by Dr Thomas Bond. In 1888, Dr Bond, who had carried out the autopsy on the Ripper's final victim, Mary Jane Kelly, also looked at the previous victims and wrote down his thoughts about the type of individual that the police should be looking for.

His report on 10 November 1888 described the following features of the murderer:

• Probably middle-aged
• Probably not in regular employment
• Physically strong
• Quiet and inoffensive in appearance; neatly and respectably dressed
• Probably lacked anatomical knowledge
• Probably solitary or a loner
• Probably eccentric or odd in behaviour

It is perhaps unsurprising to find small differences in the profiling from 1888 and 1988. At the same time, certain features in the perception of what sort of person Jack the Ripper was have remained the same.

It would seem from the expert's point of view that Jack the Ripper was an unremarkable middle-aged man and a resident of the Whitechapel area. He kept

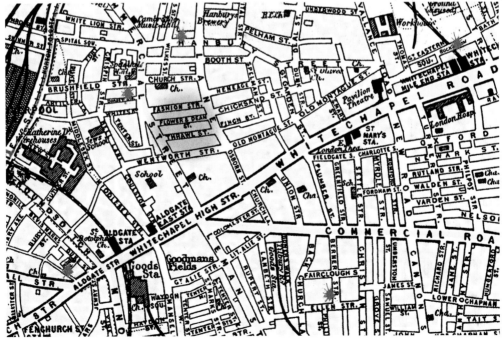

Taking the five accepted murders and using modern day geographical profiling techniques, it's possible that the killer may have lived / worked in this area of the kill zone.

himself to himself, had no real close ties with people and his behaviour, although considered odd by those who knew him, would not be enough to arouse suspicion. His brutality and hatred lay buried beneath a mask of normality until he suffered from a low bout of self-esteem and on several occasions, gave way to murder.

When faced with a criminal profile of the Ripper, it becomes clear why the police of 1888 were unable to catch him. They were searching for an obvious looking madman, but the real killer was quite the opposite. This is by no means conclusive and a profile can only take you so far.

In my own opinion the killer was clearly getting off on the acts he was committing. It was about sex and power. The bodies were displayed purposefully / intentionally, often in sexual poses. He's interested in people's reaction and the impact of what his actions will cause. He may have been cunning and calculating but he also put himself in a position where the chances of being caught were very high. Around 17 people lived at 29 Hanbury Street, coming and going at all hours. He could easily have been caught in the act. Mitre Square was patrolled every 15 minutes and, again, the killer could have been discovered during the murder. The Ripper was certainly willing to take risks. He either couldn't resist the need to kill, regardless of what might happen to him, or he was disciplined and confident. Weighing up the odds and playing them.

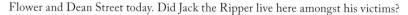

Flower and Dean Street today. Did Jack the Ripper live here amongst his victims?

Edmund Reid, one of the detectives working the case, was convinced the killer drank in the local pubs then after closing time prowled the streets, perhaps with a drunken and daring attitude. In modern times we see this in the case of the Yorkshire Ripper who would venture out to kill following several pub visits with friends. I feel this is probably the most accurate theory concerning the Ripper.

The victims also went with him of their own accord. The prostitutes who worked the streets after dark would have been wary of strangers who looked like a would-be ripper, so he must have looked like a man who would do them no harm, placing his victim at ease. It's possible he had a superficial charm about himself. Almost like the serial killer Ted Bundy. Whatever it was about him, the Ripper managed to conceal what he was until the last second, the point where sex became murder is when he showed his true intentions

In my opinion he was certainly not the criminal mastermind of legend that he is made out to be in popular culture, he was a risk taker, impulsive and irresponsible. But someone who remained undetected. 80% of that is probably due to chance and luck and 20% down to planning around what he wanted to do.

In 1998 a geographic profile was produced for the Jack the Ripper case based on five known murder sites. It's a tool used in modern crime scene investigators to pinpoint certain hot spot areas where an offender might live based on the time and locations his victims are found. When all the information was fed into the computer, the peak area of the geoprofile focused on the locale around Flower and Dean Street and Thrawl Street.

Flower and Dean Street and Thrawl Street no longer exist as they used to, but in 1888 they lay between Commercial Street to the west and Brick Lane to the east, north of Whitechapel Road; during the time of the Whitechapel murders they contained several doss houses. Dorset Street lay less than two blocks to the north along Commercial Street. This location fits perfectly with the story of the Ripper's victims, a year before their murders all of them lived within 100 yards of this street.

It would also match the route that the killer would have taken when he dropped a piece of Catherine Eddowes' apron in the doorway of Wentworth Model Dwellings, in Goulston street. This location, between Mitre Square and Flower and Dean Street, is on the likely route home if Jack the Ripper indeed lived there.

We know the police conducted house to house inquires here during the manhunt, so even they suspected the killer could reside amongst his potential victims. But sadly for us, no record survives of who they talked to, but if those names were recorded and we had them today, in that list would be Jack the Ripper. I am 99% sure they would have talked to him at some point and dismissed him as harmless and inoffensive, ordinary and mundane, exactly like the serial killers we have caught since then.

The shadow of the Ripper still lingers around the back streets and alleyways of East London. Will it remain for all time? Perhaps?

The real question is why did he stop? Killers like this seldom stop until caught, so something must have happened to bring these murders to an end.

Perhaps time and further research will reveal the name of the world's most elusive serial killer, but until it does, one thing seems certain. The legend of Jack the Ripper will continue to linger around the streets of London, and our imagination, for many years to come, and whether he was a doctor, a barrister, a prince, a pauper or perhaps some mad unknown local fiend, it's certain that his identity will remain hidden for all time, in the shadows of the Victorian night.